R

or
Perish

(With a Special Reference to
the Conservative Attack
on Hell)

John H. Gerstner

Soli Deo Gloria Publications
"...for instruction in righteousness..."

Soli Deo Gloria Publications
P.O. Box 451, Morgan, PA 15064
(412) 221-1901/FAX 221-1902

*

ISBN 1-877611-14-X

*

Repent or Perish is © 1990 by
Soli Deo Gloria Publications.
All rights reserved.

*

Third Printing 1996

CONTENTS

Foreword by Dr. John H. White	i
Chapter 1: Accidents are Not Accidental	1
Chapter 2: The Terror of the Lord	11
Chapter 3: The Conservative Revolt Against Hell	29
Chapter 4: Edward William Fudge's Particular Revolt	66
Chapter 5: Fudge On the Old Testament	100
Chapter 6: Christ's Teaching About Hell	125
Chapter 7: Paul's Teaching About Hell	163

Contents

Chapter 8: The Day of Judgment,
              Heaven and Hell   188

Chapter 9: Who are Going To Hell
              And Who To Heaven?   192

Chapter 10: How to and How Not to Repent   196

Chapter 11: Does God Love the Sinner
               And Hate Only The Sin?   208

Chapter 12: A Hard Book?   215

Foreword

Recent surveys of the future leaders of Evangelicalism reveal that close to one third of our College and Seminary students think that there may be another way to eternal salvation than through Jesus Christ (re: Evangelicalism: The Coming Generation by J.D. Hunter). The acid test of Evangelical Christian Faith has always been the absolute necessity of faith in Jesus Christ as the sole foundation for a saving relationship with God. It is frightening to read and hear of a subtle erosion of this central doctrine.

Furthermore at least two leading Evangelical theologians have recently declared publicly that they do not believe in the eternal punishment of the lost. It may be true that there are a few thinkers in the history of the Protestant Evangelical Church who have embraced annihilationism, but it has not been the predominate or Confessional (Credal) view held by the Protestant Church throughout the ages. Because of my concern as a person asked to provide leadership in the Evangelical community, I asked John Gerstner to respond, especially to John Stott and Philip Hughes in reference to the annihilation doctrine. Some of you will not like John Gerstner's forthrightness. His forte is to follow the implications of a theological point to its logical conclusion. His conclusions remind me of the disciples' response to Jesus' words in John 6, "This is a hard saying; who can hear it?" His call to his

i

Foreword

brothers to repent may be offensive to you, but my plea is that you will read with an open mind and try to move beyond an emotive response.

The Evangelical community needs the clarity, logic and forthrightness that have always been the style of John Gerstner. Dr. Gerstner, we are again indebted to you and we say — "thank you."

John H. White
President, National Association of Evangelicals
Vice President for Religious Services,
Geneva College

CHAPTER 1
ACCIDENTS ARE NOT ACCIDENTAL

Christ, at the end of the 12th chapter of Luke, was chiding the people that they could understand the signs of the coming weather but they did not grasp the far more important theological climate. We live in an age when every evening we have specialists in meteorology spelling out in great detail the national condition. They predict precisely what will confront us that evening, the next morning, and through the weekend. We are becoming ever more sophisticated reading the signs in the heavens. I fear, however, that we are even more ignorant today than in the days of Jesus about the theological climate. Whatever progress we're making in scientific sophistication is matched by theological regress.

Christ once said, *"Woe to you, Chorazin! Woe to you, Bethsaida! It will be more tolerable for Sodom and Gomorrah in the Day of Judgment than for you"* (Matt.11:21). It is not going to be tolerable for Sodom and Gomorrah in the Day of Judgment. Nothing is tolerable in hell. What Christ means is that there are degrees of torment in hell. Even the most depraved and perverted Sodomites will not suffer as terribly as people who look down their noses on sodomites, despise homosexuals, but in their own self-righteousness

Accidents Are Not Accidental

are even more wicked.

That was said by our Lord two thousand years ago. I think that if He were here today, He would be saying, "Woe to you, Pittsburgh! Woe to you, Baltimore! Woe to you, London, Paris, Berlin! It will be more tolerable for Chorazin and Bethsaida in the Day of Judgment than for you." True, we don't have the Second Person of the Godhead dwelling incarnate in our midst today. However, He has been speaking through His servants for two millennia. Our ignorance is that much more inexcusable, our judgment that much more terrible.

Christ goes on to give us specific examples of the theological climate of His day. People were not understanding that it was imperative that they settle their disputes amicably and live at peace with one another. If you don't, your opponent will *"drag you before the judge and the judge will turn you over to the constable and the constable will throw you in prison, I say to you, 'You shall not get out of there until you have paid the last cent.'"* (Luke 12:58-59) That judge was God; that prison was hell; and until you have paid the "very last cent" meant "never."

People weren't getting the message then and they are not getting it today. We rarely realize that Christ is talking about hell when He is commenting on our common relationships with one another.

The Lord speaks even more clearly in the

Accidents Are Not Accidental

parallel passage in Matthew 5, *"If you bring your gift to the altar and there recall that your brother has anything against you, leave your gift there at the altar, go first and be reconciled with your brother, and then come and offer your gift."* (vs.22-24) If we remember as we read that we have actually offended someone else and owe him an apology and recompense, we had better stop our reading immediately and go be reconciled to that brother. *"Otherwise, your opponent will hand you over to the judge, and the judge will hand you over to the guard, and you will be thrown into prison, Amen. I say to you, you will not be released until you have paid the last penny."* (vs.25-26) Here Jesus Christ is telling us that if we do not confess our sins to one another, we go to hell. There are many persons who, if they die without apologizing to those persons whom they have offended, will go immediately to hell. We sometimes mistakenly assume that relational sins are less serious than other sins. Undoubtedly, thousands at this moment are in peril of hell for that one sin of not confessing their faults to one another.

Such offenses would have to be serious. It could not be for failing to say "Good Morning." Serious offenses can be ignored only at eternal peril.

In the context of that hard saying comes the one on which we focus now. Christ was told of some Galileans who had been slain by Pilate. Probably the

Accidents Are Not Accidental

reporters had insinuated how bad the victims were that God had allowed that to happen to them. It is likely that Jesus was in Jerusalem at the time and was being told of this event by some Jerusalemites who smugly felt that all Galileans deserved such a fate. *"Can any good thing come out of Nazareth?"* Christ, reading their hearts, said that the Galileans' murder didn't imply that they were more wicked than others.

Christ didn't say that these Galileans were not sinners. He didn't say that they didn't deserve to die. He didn't say, "What a shame! Too bad! Unfair! These things will be rectified in another world. Bad things don't happen to good people." He said only one thing: this judgment did not mean that the slain were greater sinners than others, such as these reporting their deaths. *"I tell you, if you do not repent, you will all perish as they did."* (Luke 13:5) They're not the greater sinners that you think they are, nor are you free of sin and out of danger yourselves. Christ then reminds these Jews of another catastrophe that befell 18 Jerusalemites on whom a tower fell, who were no more immune to disaster than the despised Galileans.

What is the Lord teaching us here? From these two catastrophes, we learn one lesson: men who suffer disasters are not necessarily more deserving of them than those who escape them. Disaster does not prove that people are greater sinners, any more than prosperity

Accidents Are Not Accidental

proves that they are greater saints.

Venereal disease, AIDS and the like judgments usually happen to promiscuous and perverse persons. We're not talking about that type of judgment which is <u>usually</u> no accident. Also, generally speaking, prosperity does come to the godly. Righteous nations do prosper (Prov.14:34). Insofar as you are honest people, insofar as you give good service, insofar as you are reputable lawyers, doctors, teachers, and housewives, you do tend to prosper. There is no denying that.

Christ is here, however, talking about haphazard accidents. That type of thing reveals no special sinfulness in the person to whom it happens, or sinlessness of those to whom it does not happen. The lesson is simply that the victims are not greater sinners, nor are the spared ones greater saints.

All men deserve to suffer disaster. Jesus doesn't say that in so many words. It is between His lines. It is in His Bible as a whole, including His own statement in John 8:34, *"he who commits sin is a slave of sin."* Who doesn't commit sin? Therefore, all of us are or were slaves. What are the wages of sin? Eternal death (Rom.6:23). Every solitary one of us, every solitary fellow human being is fit for hell. It is an act of divine mercy that a child lives three days, three weeks, three years. It is an act of divine mercy that a child lives three

Accidents Are Not Accidental

seconds. We are under the condemnation of Adam in whom we fell (Rom.5:12).

We need to remember this all the days we live, no matter who we are. In and of ourselves, we deserve hell. If we remember that every one of us in this world, no one of us excepted, not even Jesus Christ, deserves anything other than hell. Christ deserved it also because He took our guilt upon Himself. We deserve it because we have incurred our own guilt.

If you recognize that basic Christian teaching, you'll understand why I wrote a little primer entitled "The Problem of Pleasure." We talk so much about the Problem of Pain. There's no such thing as the problem of pain! You tell me how excruciating it is and I'll still look you in the face and say there's no problem. Why? Because we're sinners. We deserve the eternal wrath of God. I don't care who you are or where you are. That you are breathing at all is incredibly gracious. What needs explaining is not that there's pain in the world. If there wasn't any pain, we would have a problem.

How can God be holy and this world be wholly sinful and there be anything but pain? It's incredible that there is non-pain. All of us, even Christian theologians, are wrestling constantly with the problem of pain. Where did we get the idea that there was a problem of pain? You don't find too many people

Accidents Are Not Accidental

wrestling with the problem of pleasure. But that is the problem. Why does any of us draw a free breath? Why does any person not have a heart attack? Why is anybody not suffering? That's a problem!

Christ solves that problem. Temporary freedom from pain is given you so that you may repent and not perish. The only answer to the problem of pleasure is that God is pleased to give hell-deserving sinners an opportunity to repent. That is the only reason anybody lives a moment out of hell - that he may escape hell forever.

So the suffering of some is not a call to condemn them but to condemn all, especially ourselves. We must all repent. Christ is telling us that when disaster, tragedy, suffering, or accidents happen to some we are all to get the message: repent or perish. Accidents are not accidental. They are God's way of screaming at people who pay no attention to conscience, nor His Word. They go through life complaining of how much they have to suffer, of how much they are deprived. They are constantly distressed with this, that, and the other. They never, for a moment, seriously consider what they deserve. Pain is God's way of shaking us up to the problem of pleasure.

People who pay no attention to the Bible, or religion, or conscience can really be "shook up" by having someone in the family die. In my own pastoral

Accidents Are Not Accidental

experience, a disfigured child was born to a Christian couple. I knew I had to call. It was a very hard visit. I asked God to give me the grace to deal with this suffering couple, to weep with those who weep. When I came to the door, I wasn't just Jack Gerstner, their personal friend. I was John Gerstner, pastor of the church, representative of their God. All the indignation they had stored up against God they poured on me: "How could God do this to US?" They were evangelical people. They were active church members. They were outstanding, zealous members of my congregation saying, "How could God do this to US?" Since my friends were angry with God, I was pleased that they took it out on me, His servant. I sat them down on the couch and asked them what they thought they deserved. In spite of all their evangelical protestations, all their singing "nothing in my hand I bring, simply to Thy cross I cling," did they really believe they were people who deserved better treatment? That a fair and just God couldn't possibly do this to THEM? Thank God, they did what they ought. They became ashamed of themselves instead of God and His servant. They were penitent. They asked God to forgive them, and I'm sure He did forgive them.

My point is this, can any of us, live under the supposition that we don't really deserve the heavy hand of God? Do we think we're pretty good people?

Accidents Are Not Accidental

Not sinners saved by grace after all? God shook that couple. When this type of thing occurs, people think, in many cases for the first time, seriously about God.

If we do not repent, we shall perish eternally just as these accident victims perished temporally. Christ can't mean that unless we repent we are going to have a tower fall on us. Christ must mean that "unless you repent, you're going to perish forever."

That shouldn't surprise us. We have been told that we were born dead in trespasses and sins, under the wrath of God. If we die unchanged, we are going to die forever under His wrath. God is shaking us up by these accidents that aren't accidental. If we do not remember that, death can come any moment and find us not ready except for hell.

So here is our solemn warning, friends. When accidents befall, God is screaming at us. Accidents are not accidental. We're going to get as much food as possible to the starving in Ethiopia, wherever. Nevertheless, many of them are dying. They haven't sinned more than we that this is happening to them. Everyone of them who dies cries out to us, "Unless you repent, you will also die eternally." Not necessarily by starvation. You're going to suffer death more terrible than starvation. You're going to die eternally in the flames of hell.

If we do repent as we are admonished to do, then

Accidents Are Not Accidental

there's no such thing as disaster. I was speaking at a university conference sometime ago, and a coed asked me, "What is tragedy?" I answered, "Tragedy is anything that happens to an impenitent person. It never, ever happens to a penitent person." Tragedy is everything that happens to an impenitent person but never happens to a penitent one. It never happens to a penitent person because his sins have been taken away and everything that God ordains, no matter how severe it is, makes him say, "I don't have a pain to spare. I wouldn't have it any other way. This is God's ordaining and is going to do me good." For the Christian, the word "tragedy" doesn't exist. But for a non-Christian, pleasure is a tragedy. Prosperity is tragedy, unmitigated tragedy. What is meant to give you an opportunity to turn away from wrath and start storing up treasures in heaven, you use to heap up more wrath. If you're out of Christ and impenitent, your whole life, not only its sad but its happy moments, is tragic.

If you do not repent, you must face the terror of the Lord.

CHAPTER 2
THE TERROR OF THE LORD

Paul preached: *"Knowing therefore the terror of the Lord we persuade men."* (2 Cor.5:11) I am constantly impressed that we hear <u>little or nothing</u> of the terror of the Lord except in some fundamentalistic groups. By contrast, in Jonathan Edwards' Northampton congregation (1726-1750), where there was little or no open or gross vice, the people heard of it, constantly being warned that all were in danger of hell unless they were born again. In one sermon preached in May 1741, for example, he said: "I don't desire to go about to terrify you needlessly or represent your case worse than it is, but I do verily think that there are a number of people belonging to this congregation in imminent danger of being damned to all eternity."

I have been reading in "Dear Abby," as well as her sister and many other pop counselors, of the numerous reports of promiscuous sex in many college dormitories today. The parents who wrote protested the veritable brothel conditions not befitting disreputable hotels. That such behavior guaranteed eternal damnation is never reported by the counsellors. The "terror of the Lord" does not exist for our culture generally, in spite of the wide-spread profession of belief in God. Yet someone has written that if God does not judge us,

The Terror of the Lord

He will have to apologize to Sodom and Gomorrah.

Very recently a Gallup poll listed the percentage of students who engaged in promiscuous sex: the percentage of Roman Catholics, the percentage of Protestants, and the percentage of evangelical students. Even approximately twenty percent of evangelicals think they can be evangelical and live in disobedience to Christ. The terror of the Lord doesn't even frighten them. America's best known business man, Donald Trump, alleges the corrupt maneuvering for personal gain of most of the very rich. Fear of the Lord seems to be nowhere evident in high finance.

In sophisticated religious journals, the terror of the Lord comes in only if it is the subject of some research (usually trying to downplay it). It is not surprising that one of my typists (a conservative Christian herself), doing work for me on Jonathan Edwards, found him "stuck in some kind of rut" on the hell theme. Once I preached a half-hour sermon on "The Love of Enemies" in which I made a one-sentence reference to hell. A parishioner on the way out said we ought to hear more sermons like that about hell!

Surely if Christianity be true, Christians everywhere will be trying to persuade their friends to avoid the terror of the Lord. If they are never doing so, is it conceivable that they are Christians themselves?

Knowing only Christ and Him crucified is the

The Terror of the Lord

corollary of knowing the terror of the Lord and persuading men. The only thing that will save women and men from the terror of the Lord is the cross of the Lord. But it is usually the terror of the Lord that first brings them to consider the cross of the Lord. If men do not fear the terror of the Lord they must experience that terror. If you are not afraid of hell, you are almost certainly going there. You will then never doubt it again.

Is it conceivable that there are Christians who do not believe in hell? Some think they are Christians precisely because they reject hell! Their God could never send human beings to eternal torment, they say. Their God would be in eternal torment if He did that to one human wretch, or, as some say, to a dog. So it is hardly conceivable to them that men are Christians who <u>do</u> believe in hell. However, their God, who is incapable of inflicting such punishment, is not the God and Father of Jesus Christ who teaches hell as do His appointed apostles.

How do you persuade men? If you prove hell to sinful men, you persuade them to flee from it. Why, then, was John the Baptist cynical about the multitudes who fled the wrath of God?

> *Then said he to the multitude that came forth to be baptized of him, O generation of*

The Terror of the Lord

vipers, who hath warned you to flee from the wrath to come? Bring forth therefore fruits worthy of repentance, and begin not to say within yourselves, We have Abraham to our father: for I say unto you, That God is able of these stones to raise up children unto Abraham. And now also the axe is laid to the root of the trees: every tree therefore which brings not forth good fruit is hewn down and case into the fire.

They apparently believed in hell. Why was John cynical? Because they thought that they were not sinful men and had no need to flee. Men usually think they are not sinful ("We have Abraham to our father"). They do what is right in their eyes, Judges 17:6. What they do is right. Why should the terror of the Lord terrify those who are righteous? Because, said John, you are not righteous as you think. How do you know, John, since they say that they are? Ought they not to know about themselves better than you? John: what they are claiming is righteousness stinks.

If there is no bad news there cannot be any good news. The good news is deliverance from the bad news. We are all born on the road to destruction. The good news is that we can be delivered from it. If you do not believe you are on the way to hell, how can you

The Terror of the Lord

be interested in the good news of deliverance from it?

Look at "salvation" today. It is freedom from life's frustrations. We are saved from our narrowness and anxieties. We learn to live with doubts and fears. We take pills to relieve our pressures. That's our gospel. Ann Landers is our savior and, if she can't do her job, her sister will. Or if you have more educated sicknesses, get the local psychiatrist.

What a day! Take hell. Take heaven. Take sin. Take salvation. Children's games. Most of what we think and do are diversions from a real hell to which all out of Christ are moving steadily and moving relentlessly. No doubt, horror books and movies are popular with many because they are fictional substitutes for their discarded real hell. In comparison with the real hell, Stephen King's most frightening tales are amusing. <u>Christ tells us most about hell, and He is the one we use to assure ourselves that there is no hell</u>. The true Jesus warns us that if we do not repent we will surely perish, but He is made to say that God is our heavenly Father whether we repent or not, whether we are true Christians or not.

Many want little pagan children in public schools to say "Our Father who art in heaven..." while their father is in hell, and they are on their way to join their father unless they repent. Jesus said to the most orthodox religious leaders of His day: *"you generation of*

The Terror of the Lord

vipers, how can you escape the damnation of hell?" (Matt.23:33) We let everyone, including irreligious, wicked persons (whose only use for Christ is to provide a profane vocabulary), escape the damnation of hell. Indeed, we assure them that there is no hell no matter how much they deserve it. All this and annihilation, too.

Christ tells us <u>not to fear those who can destroy the body</u>, but *"fear Him who can destroy body and soul in hell."* (Matt.10:28) We fear the mafia, and even the boss who can only take our job and not our life, but God? Who is afraid of God?

The only one we should fear is the One we never do fear. God may not even be, but if He is, one thing is sure, He need never be feared. "God-fearing" is a bad word today. He could not send anyone to hell even if He wanted to. His mercy has His hands of holy wrath tied behind His back. Fear Him who can destroy the body (that's the only hell there ever is), but never, never fear God who cannot destroy the soul, not to mention the body, not to think of "in hell." All this is constantly being said in the name of Jesus Christ.

Christ warns men of the hell where *"the worm dies not and the fire is not quenched,"* (Mark 9:44, 46). For contemporary Christians, Christ's hell-preaching is not "Christian." The church of Christ simply will not let Christ say such things; the fact that He does,

The Terror of the Lord

notwithstanding.

Don't act from fear of punishment or desire of reward, men say. Act morally, men say. Do not consider consequences, men say. Don't be afraid of hell or desirous of heaven, men say. <u>How unethical Christ is</u> who teaches us to lay up treasure in heaven (Matt.6:20), and, to make matters worse, asks: *"what does it <u>profit</u> a man if he gains the whole world and loses his soul?"* (Mark 8:36)

Rewards and punishments - the destruction of true morality, say the ethicists. The foundations of it, says Jesus Christ. If you do things to avoid punishment or gain praise, you are not doing things because they are right, but because of their consequences. You are not acting for virtue's sake but for what you get out of virtue. Not for virtue but for virtue's rewards, not for God but for what God gives you. If God gave you nothing, you would not love Him, and if the devil gave you rewards, you would worship him.

Strangely, Christ says the same thing. Those who claimed to have done "mighty works" in His name, He dismissed as not being "known" by Him (Matt.7:23). They had done these mighty works in His name for rewards in the Day of Judgment, but not for His sake. So they received no reward but only punishment. They had not laid up treasure in heaven but punishment in hell.

The Terror of the Lord

Christ had told them to work for reward and to avoid punishment and they had not done so. You say, that is just what they did do and Christ disowned them. He seems to have rejected His own ethic.

Not quite. Christ taught that what ever is done *"in His name"* (Mark 9:41) has its rewards. So if a person is interested in reward, he will act in Christ's name. He aims at Christ's name (or glory), not at reward, and he receives both. He aims at reward and not Christ's glory and he receives neither.

That is Christ's ethic, but rarely today is it the "Christian" ethic, even among the sophisticates.

Jesus Christ was a "scare" theologian. He was not afraid of making people afraid. It was Paul's knowing the terror of the Lord that led him to persuade people to seek the Lord. The Lord was not only a Scare Preacher, but He is the One of whom people should be afraid. He is an angry God and He has the whole world in His hands. So when Jonathan Edwards preached about "Sinners in the Hands of an Angry God," he was only echoing His Lord.

What is wrong with scare preaching? The reason people give for condemning scare preaching, in which their Lord engaged, is usually that frightened people will say or do whatever the threatener asks, regardless of their personal convictions. Scare preaching makes hypocrites of people, or cowards. If we are afraid of

The Terror of the Lord

hell, we will do or say anything the threatener requires to escape going there. But what is wrong with doing what the <u>divine</u> Threatener requires? The Judge of heaven and earth cannot do or command anything evil. Whatever He requires is good and proper to do.

Human terrorists use their threats to make you say or do what is against conscience and ought not to be done. So you must resist their threats to the death. It is a sin to fear their threats, Matt.10:28a, as it is a sin not to fear divine threats, Matt.10:28b. However, even some human threateners do so in the name of God, Rom.13:1, and have the same right so to do as God Himself, whom they represent. When the state threatens jail, or worse, for various crimes, it acts under God's authority. Citizens are to obey it not only for the sword's sake, but *"for conscience's sake,"* Rom.13:5. Parents and other authorities have the same right under God to threaten and to punish.

What does the divine Threatener require to avoid hell, which, as sinners, we all deserve? He commands us to believe on the Lord Jesus Christ and be saved! In other words, the divine Threatener provides the damned with a way of salvation and "threatens" them with what is their due if they do not accept His grace which is not their due. Was there ever such a benign threat?

True, you say, but just the same, those who are terrified will say they believe in Christ just to escape

The Terror of the Lord

hell. Anything to escape hell. Even profess to accept grace for no other reason than to escape hell. People are driven insane with such fear.

But <u>saying</u> you believe in Christ is not what God requires. <u>Saying</u> one believes in Christ never saved anyone from hell. In fact, merely <u>saying</u> one believes in Christ only to escape hell damns hypocrites to a yet hotter hell. So how can <u>saying</u> you believe merely to escape from hell ever help you escape hell? And if it doesn't, then scare preaching does not produce a hypocritical, cowardly saying anything to escape the threat. As for terror driving people mad, it drives them to sanity. For sinners to eat, drink, and be merry while such living daily heats their hell the more is insane. Scare preaching awakens them to sanity and possible salvation.

What does scare preaching really produce? It produces an awesome, trembling awareness that you must have saving (not saying) faith in Christ. So the frightened ones will try sincerely to believe in Christ and be saved, which is what they ought to do for the glory of God, for the good of their own souls, and for the avoiding of deserved perdition.

When they try truly and soberly to believe in Christ, they discover, to their horror, it is not in them to do so. This is what Christ had been telling them all along. *"This is the condemnation that light is come*

The Terror of the Lord

into the world and men loved the darkness rather than the light." (John 3:19) Christ is the Light of the world and these needy sinners hate all light, hate the Light especially, whom they must love (as they ought), if they would be saved!

If they must believe to be saved and they do not have this faith, and cannot have it when their own hearts hate Christ, where in the world are they to get it? Nowhere in the world or in themselves. Where, then? Only from God Himself. Only from the Threatener Himself! Only by His - if He pleases to bestow it - sovereign mercy!

The evangelistic situation is this:
1. The sinner is threatened with the horrible hell he so justly deserves unless he accepts Christ's undeserved salvation.
2. But he hates the Christ who alone can save him.
3. That hatred can only be removed, and a believing heart bestowed in its place, by sovereign divine mercy.
4. So the sinner must seek God's mercy, which will come, if God pleases, only by divine regeneration.

The effect of biblical scare preaching is, therefore, to set a sinner seeking salvation, and not saying he has found it until he has. He will not lie to save himself, knowing that would only aggravate his damnation. As

The Terror of the Lord

a sinner set in the ways of sin, he is very unlikely to seek God at all unless he is afraid not to. No one is ever scared into heaven, but very few have ever gone to heaven who have not first been afraid of going to hell. In a word, scare preaching is to produce: not salvation, but the seeking of salvation.

Granted that impenitent, mature sinners must be shown the terror of the Lord. What about children and church members? None of these should be threatened if there is reason to believe that they have been born again, for in Christ Jesus there is no condemnation, Rom.8:1-3, no hell. *"There is therefore now no condemnation to them which are in Christ Jesus, who walk not after the flesh, but after the Spirit. For the law of the Spirit of life in Christ Jesus hath made me free from the law of sin and death. For what the law could not do, in that it was weak through the flesh, God sending His own Son in the likeness of sinful flesh, and for sin, condemned sin in the flesh."*

But being a child, or being a church member, is no proof that one is born again. Knowing the terror of the Lord, we should try to persuade both to seek the Lord. In fact, no period of life is so hopeful as the first period. Children are much more likely to believe their parents, pastors, and friends than when they become older; except, perhaps, when they are on their deathbed (when it's often too late to seek God).

The Terror of the Lord

Why, then, do so many vehemently oppose frightening children? They don't. They scare children away from fire, from electric sockets, from poisonous drinks or pills, from snakes, from certain toys, from anything that threatens them.

Why, then, do almost all seem to oppose frightening children with hell? The answer is obvious: they wrongly fancy that children are not in danger of hell. Can you imagine that a mother who would give her own life to save her child's wouldn't do everything to save her child from hell if she knew there was any danger?

There are three imagined reasons for supposing that children are in no danger of hell. Some think children are innocent of sin and guilt. Some admit that they are not innocent, but are saved from sin by being born again in infant baptism. Some fancy that though little sinners, not regenerated in baptism, children are, nonetheless, safe in the covenant of grace.

Infants are not innocent, but born in guilt and sin. Paul says we were all born dead in trespasses and sins, Eph.2:1. In Adam, in whom children are born, all died, Rom.5:12. Only *"in Christ* (in whom all need to be reborn), *are all made alive."* (1 Cor.15:22) So until children are born again, they are in imminent peril of eternal damnation and should be made aware of it as soon as possible.

The Terror of the Lord

This is not to deny that some infants may have been born again even in the womb before they have been born into this world. That seems to be true of John the Baptist (Luke 1:41) and Jeremiah (Jeremiah 1:5). We only know that, however, from divine revelation. There is no such revelation for all children. We must assume that they have not been born again, since we do not know that they have been and we do know that they are conceived dead, Ps.51:5. In any and all cases, no infant was ever born <u>innocent</u> except the Virgin-born One.

I may relate here my experience with a church which asked me if I - in the absence of a resident pastor - would baptize a child of two of their members. I assured them I would be happy to do so. Then I was asked if I minded following the congregation's practice of using a white carnation with which to apply the water. Rather than saying that I did mind, I asked the elder, "What is the meaning of the white carnation?" He explained that it is to "show the child's innocence." I then asked, "What is the meaning of the water?" He explained that it is to symbolize the washing away of the child's sin - but he couldn't finish the sentence, realizing the absurdity. How could one use a symbol of innocence to apply the symbol of guilt and cleansing? Children are not innocent, but guilty by nature as their parents before them. And the wages of sin is

The Terror of the Lord

eternal death, Rom.6:23. Children must be warned as we lovingly teach them "their lost condition by nature."

Infant baptism does not bring regeneration. Children's guilt is not washed away by water as natural dirt is. Since the Protestant Church almost everywhere denies baptismal regeneration, I think it unnecessary to prove it here where space is at a premium.

Some Reformed people are, however, inclined to believe that the covenant of grace, made between God and believers, includes the election of the believer's children. One Reformed theologian, however, who heard of Jonathan Edwards' referring to his unconverted children (virtually all of whom, incidentally, were in youth wonderfully converted), as "little vipers," reacted strongly saying, "They may be little vipers, but they are in 'covenantal diapers.'" He did not explain, but apparently meant that though covenant children are born as little sinners, they are born in the covenant of grace.

I cannot here enter into a discussion of covenant theology in relation to infants of professed believers. Sufficient to say that descendancy from Christians does not guarantee the genes of faith. Ishmael and Isaac were both descended from Abraham. Both were circumcised, according to covenant. One later had faith. The other never did. Jacob and Esau were both

The Terror of the Lord

descended from Isaac. Both were circumcised, according to covenant. One later had faith. The other never did. All children of a believer are "holy" (1 Cor. 7:14). All are baptized. Some later have faith. Others never do.

It is clear that all children are born dead in sin and must be assumed to continue such, facing the "terror of the Lord" until they are born again. Parents, pastors, and all Christians are obliged to seek salvation for and with them until they clearly believe or clearly refuse to believe. There is no single person, except the one who is clearly converted by God or damned forever by the unpardonable sin, who should not be persuaded of the terror of the Lord, as well as the possible mercy of the Lord.

The best-known and best-hated sermon in American history is "Sinners in the Hands of an Angry God." It was one of Edwards' less terrifying sermons. There is no record of its awesome effects when it was first preached in Northampton, the home church; but only when repeated by the itinerating Edwards in Enfield, Connecticut, July 8, 1741.

Surely "The Justice of God in the Damnation of Sinners" was more frightening, and Edwards himself thought that God had honored it more in its effects. I find Matthew 25:46's sermon, in which Edwards annihilated annihilation and goes into detail about

The Terror of the Lord

what the Lord means when He says "These shall go away into everlasting punishment" more terrible, and the Romans 2:4 sermon dealing with the heaping up of wrath in this world for the judgment in the next the most terrible of all.

The great contemporary effort to introduce Edwards to the learned by the learned does not deny the minatory sermons, but hastily tries to show the cultured despisers of Calvinism that there was more to Edwards' preaching than God the Holy Terror.

Edwards got heat in his own generation for his hell-fire preaching. He had to ask his generation, as we ours, don't you warn people when their house is on fire to get out or be burned alive? Is that so unfriendly? Of course, that was the problem with some then and almost all now: they cannot believe that their spiritual house is on fire.

Edwards proved it to them then and, thanks to his "cultured despisers," is trying to prove it to us today. The Yale University Press publication of his Works is getting some highly educated people to read the fiery Puritan who would not "waste their time" other-wise.

As a matter of fact, possibly Edwards was most frightening when he stopped preaching for a few minutes and addressed the doubters in his own congregation. He would say something like this: "There are some among you who do not believe the Bible when

The Terror of the Lord

it says these awful things about hell. Let me show you that reason teaches the same doctrine." Then the finest philosopher-theologian in American history would prove it to their secular minds as they sat brazen or sank frozen into their hard pews.

Was Edwards a "scare preacher?" Of course. Was he hoping to scare people into the Kingdom of God? Of course not. Why, then, the scare preaching? Two reasons: 1. God, in His Word, is a Scare Preacher; 2. The fear of hell is the only thing most likely to get worldly people thinking about the Kingdom of God. No rational human being can be convinced that he is in imminent danger of everlasting torment and do nothing about it. But, you say, there are many now, and were even in Edwards' day, who fear hell, or say they do, and yet don't believe or seek the gift of faith. That is true, but, as we say, that only proves that they are no longer "rational human beings."

Did Edwards' scare theology get worldly people thinking about the Kingdom of God? More than that. It got them seeking the Kingdom of God.

CHAPTER 3
THE CONSERVATIVE REVOLT AGAINST HELL

Most people who are going to hell find it more comfortable to deny that fact than admit it. Yet denying hell is one of the main reasons they are going there. God can't lie Himself, and can't stand the company of liars.

Their enemies assure them that they are not going to hell. Their friends warn them that they are. Foolishly, they make their enemies friends for telling them lies. They make their friends enemies for telling them the truth, though with the kind of friends they have, they need no enemies.

Pathetic as it is that most people deny hell, it is not surprising. That many conservative Christians, who traditionally have believed and preached the awesome doctrine, now are denying it, is amazing. When liberals deny hell, that is to be expected. When "fundamentalists" do, that stops ecclesiastical traffic.

The reason for the surprise is that the source of Christian conviction about hell, the Bible, has not changed, but the convictions have. Heaven and hell have been two virtually unquestioned doctrines of the Bible since the Christian church began. East and West, Roman and Protestant have differences on many

The Conservative Revolt Against Hell

doctrines, but not on these. In fact, the denial of hell, until recently, has been the usual litmus test of a cult such as Jehovah's Witnesses, Christian Science, Mormonism, New Thought, New Age, Seventh-day Adventism, and Liberalism; especially Liberalism.

I mentioned Liberalism (or Modernism) last, though it is the most important cult, because it is a parasite on denominations rather than a denomination. There are probably many more anti-supernaturalist, anti-miracle members of the orthodox churches than orthodox members; but, they do not express themselves credally. They are parasites who cannot exist apart from a live evangelical church. As C.H. Spurgeon once wrote, liberalism could never build a matchbox, much less a cathedral.

Liberalism never has had any truck with hell in this world. It doesn't believe in a supernatural salvation, much less supernatural damnation. The never-silent majority has always been against hell because it has always been against Christianity.

On the other hand, or at the other end of church members, the conservatives hold most tenaciously to orthodox dogmas. They believe in hell, teach it to their children, and try to save their acquaintances from it because they believe in Christianity.

The great middle of the church are like the conservatives in tacitly believing Orthodoxy. They are like

The Conservative Revolt Against Hell

the liberals, on the other hand, in being apathetic about them.

So we are not surprised at liberal unbelief in hell, or the average Christian's slight concern beyond acceptance, but amazed when we learn of "The Conservative Attack on Hell." No conservative wants to seem to rejoice in eternal torment. It is as awesome for him as for anyone - perhaps more so because he takes it so seriously and sees it as so inevitable for the wicked. He dreads it and seeks to be delivered from it, and deliver others as well. It breaks his heart to see people perish by the thousands around him daily, even though it never comes near his own soul.

He holds tenaciously to the doctrine for one essential reason: God's Word teaches it. If God teaches it, hell is true and right and good. The evangelical cannot contemplate hell without horror because of the awfulness of its eternal torments. But shrink from it as he may, he cannot deny it because to deny hell for the Bible-believer is to deny God. To believe in hell is awful. To deny God is impossible. *"Master, to whom shall we go? You have the words of eternal life"* (John 6:68). If the evangelical will hold to God, he knows he must hold to hell. If he parts will hell, he knows he parts with Jesus Christ, his God and Savior. If he loves God, he must love hell, too. If God decrees it, it must be good and for God's glory, and the evangelical

The Conservative Revolt Against Hell

knows that he will sing God's praises eternally as the smoke ascends from the burning pit! AMEN!

Even <u>now</u> while the evangelical is singing the praises of his Lord and Savior, Jesus Christ, he knows that multitudes are suffering the torments of the damned. He knows that Judas Iscariot has been in unimaginable agony of soul for two thousand years, and that the worst of all torments will be that after his buried body is raised from his bones and ashes he will suffer in body and soul forever and ever. The true Christian, aware of this, is happily, exuberantly, gladly praising the Judge of the Last Day, Jesus Christ, who has sentenced to such merited damnation millions of souls.

So a conservative attack on hell is almost unbelievable. It <u>is</u> unbelievable. Before this book is over I hope to have shown that when a conservative believer attacks hell, he has ceased to be a conservative believer, if a believer at all. When Christ asks, "Do you love Me?" He is asking also "Do you love hell?" When a Christian prays, "Hallowed by Thy name," he reverences God's punishing the impenitent everlastingly. If this *"is life eternal that they know thee the only true God and Jesus Christ whom He has sent,"* (John 17:3), then eternal life means loving a God who keeps hell eternally burning.

Of course, the conservative attack on hell is not

The Conservative Revolt Against Hell

entirely new in the United States. Though the original founders were Roman Catholics and Protestant denominations which propagated traditional general orthodoxy, before the eighteenth century was over, the first conservative attack on hell was under way.

If the greatest preacher of hell was Jonathan Edwards, his chief opponent, Charles Chauncy of First Church, Boston (1727-1787), may have been the first unofficial universalist. This doctrine was then so heretical that Chauncy did not dare proclaim it but kept his writing on the subject secret (known to friends as the "pudding" until it was finally published anonymously). All universalists deny hell, of course. However, one does not need to be a universalist to deny hell as the erstwhile evangelical John Stott will insist later in this chapter.

It was 1803 before the Winchester Platform declared the ultimate salvation of all men. During the first half of last century the eschatological battle raged. By the end of the century, Universalism was established and its break with Orthodoxy settled. By 1961 it had united with Unitarianism, showing clearly that its break with hell was at heart a break with biblical Christianity.

Universalism, with its denial of hell, became identified with Liberalism's general unbelief. As such it has simply been a part of Liberalism's anti-

The Conservative Revolt Against Hell

supernaturalism, which denies bodily resurrection and is uncertain, if not opposed, to <u>any</u> doctrine of future life. Orthodoxy continued to proclaim, however infrequently, the traditional doctrine until the current conservative attack on hell and in spite of it.

There was a famous near debate between two conservatives, Henry Ward Beecher and William G.T.Shedd, that anticipated the break at the end of the nineteenth century. When Beecher read Shedd's case vindicating eternal punishment, he wired: "Cancel engagement, Shedd is too much for me. I half believe in eternal punishment now myself. Get somebody else." The article was never written and Dr. Shedd remained unanswered (A.H.Strong, <u>Systematic Theology</u>, 1052-1053).

However, the three greatest theologians of the turn of the century, the Presbyterians, Shedd and Charles Hodge, and the Baptist, Augustus Hopkins Strong, held to Orthodoxy in general, including the doctrine of hell. When compared with Jonathan Edwards, however, there was a slight slippage in conservative Strong.

This century's radical Christian neo-orthodox scholars have no use for hell. Radical scholars, of course, have no use for hell. Rudolf Bultmann rejected the future, not just a never-ending miserable future. For him, all New Testament hell texts were

The Conservative Revolt Against Hell

the work of some sinister redactor. Dietrich Bonhoeffer did not need the "hypothesis" of God, much less the notion of any sinners in His angry hands. Paul Tillich did not believe in a personal God, so hell was out of the question, though before Tillich died, he tended to fear that there may be a devil because there is so very much evil in this world (to which he made no minor contribution himself).

To note the conservative attack, let us begin with a couple of encyclopedias. One would never get the impression, not to mention the information, that the historic, orthodox doctrine of hell is a place of unending torment of body and soul from <u>The New International Dictionary of the Christian Church</u>, (Third Printing, 1979) article on "Hell." I next checked the <u>Oxford Dictionary of the Church</u> (First Edition, 1957, and Second Edition, 1974) to see if there was any significant change in the articles on our subject. In 1957:

> It is clear that in the N.T., Hell in this sense is an ultimate state or destiny into which souls pass only by God's final and irrevocable judgement, whether that is conceived as the *Particular Judgement at death or the *General Judgement on the last day. Acc. to the traditional Scholastic theology, souls experience in Hell both the *poena damni*, i.e. the exclusion from God's presence and loss of all contact with Him, and a certain *poena sensus*,

The Conservative Revolt Against Hell

> denoted in the Bible by fire, which is usually interpreted as an external agent. The fact that Hell is but the logical consequence of ultimate adherence to the soul's own will, and rejection of the will of God, which (since God cannot take away free will) necessarily separates the soul from God, and hence from all possibility of happiness. This exclusion from Heaven (in which the unrepentant person would, from his very character, be both unable and unwilling to share) is held to be contrary neither to God's justice nor to His love, since He will not force response to the good from any creature against his will.

The 1974 second edition reads: "Modern theology tends rather to stress the fact that Hell is but the logical consequence of ultimate adherence to the soul's own will and rejection of the will of God, which (since God cannot take away free will) necessarily separates the soul from God, and hence from all possibility of happiness." Hell seems to be merely "exclusion from heaven...."

Of course, the generally conservative Seventh-Day Adventists have had the courage of their wrong convictions about hell. LeRoy Froom wrote his massive volume The Conditionalist Faith of Our Fathers, 2 volumes (1965), trying to show that the S.D.A.'s were orthodox in their heresy. But Froom was better at gathering superficial statistics than penetrating analy-

The Conservative Revolt Against Hell

sis that makes much of his research much less valuable than it appears to be. That some of the church Fathers were heretical on the subject of hell Froom shows, but the unfaith of the Fathers as a class he does not demonstrate. That S.D.A. Ralph Blodgett wrote against hell in 1982 is not surprising, but that his writing was published in the conservative Eternity magazine, and that he stated his error in a way approaching the unpardonable sin was ("Hell as professionally believed and taught is the doctrine of the devil and not of God.").

Roman Catholicism has been a hot bed of unbelief in spite of the church's official orthodox eschatological standards (only heaven and hell are eternal). Most everyone knows that Pope John Paul II is a virtual universalist, so it is not so unexpected that lesser Romanists would deviate from strict Romish Orthodoxy. I have not noticed anything recently, even in Andrew Greely, that matches the flagrancy of Robert Short's Something to Believe In. He does not hesitate to trace to the hell doctrine the cruelty of the Inquisition and the atheism of Richard Wagner and Friederich Nietzche, and notes that Freudianism may have been induced by a governess who terrified Sigmund as a child with tales of hell. Karl Rahner in Sacramentum Mundi, volume 3, after eliminating external fire, also asserts that "eternity" is not the continued duration of time after the history of freedom...."(8) Of course,

The Conservative Revolt Against Hell

there have been Roman defenders of Roman Orthodoxy such as the late Bishop Fulton Sheen.

Probably the most heard and read of modern Lutherans is Martin Marty, and his denial of hell has been typically eloquent ("Whatever Happened to Hell?" in The Lutheran, 4/2/86). For the Rev. Du Sean Berkich, "Hell Was a Dump near Jerusalem." On "The Cultural Unavailability of Hell fire and Brimstone" (Religion and Society, 2/87), he used the insignificance of hell today as undermining any real value of prayer in public schools as a way of social control. Frederick Niedner assured his Valparaiso University audience that even Judas was not in hell, and Richard John Neuhaus goes further in his droll confidence that hell exists, but no one is in it. Classical Lutherans such as Kant, Schleiermacher, and Ritschl were universalists while Theodor Zahn dismissed hell as mere superstition. In the midst of all this unbelief, stalwart Lutherans hold firm to Scripture, Martin Luther, and their standards, citing, among others, the Augsburg Confession of 1530, XVII, "they condemn the Anabaptists, who think that there will be an end to the punishment of condemned men and devils." Christian News approvingly cites J.T. Mueller, one of the great Missouri Synod theologians who spelled out the orthodox doctrine with scholastic precision.

Steven H. Travis' I Believe in the Second Coming

The Conservative Revolt Against Hell

of Jesus (Eerdmans, 1982), was a significant conservative straw in the wind of unbelief, because it was part of a series by noted evangelical, Michael Green. Travis found the evidence for Orthodoxy or for Annihilation not compelling on either side. However, as far as he was concerned, it seemed that the case against Orthodoxy was compelling enough, especially when a non-argument such as this counted with him: 1 Cor. 15:28 teaches that God would be all in all, and this could not be if heaven and hell existed alongside each other!

Speaking generally, Donald Bloesch, in his Essence of Evangelical Theology (1979), Volume II, p.211, notes that heaven and hell have virtually disappeared from evangelical preaching. James P. Martin's title, The Last Judgment in Protestant Theology from Orthodoxy to Ritschl (1963), seems to indicate his own theological slide. One of the very latest scholarly attacks on the orthodoxy of hell is found in McIntyre's "Jesus' Teaching on Hell." He sees hades used as sheol and sheol as grave. In the spirit of Edward William Fudge, he remarks that Christ's gehenna results in complete destruction (Henceforth... 1988).

Of course, modern times have known conservative defenses of biblical hell. Many rank and file ministers have been faithful in their pulpits. Books have appeared. It was in 1979 that Jon E. Braun

The Conservative Revolt Against Hell

published his <u>Whatever Happened to Hell</u>? (Nelson). Harry Buis' <u>The Doctrine of Eternal Punishment</u> (1957) is recognized by Fudge as a fine work defending the orthodox doctrine. Roger Nicole spoke for Orthodoxy in "The Punishment of the Wicked" (<u>Christianity Today</u>, 9 June, 1958).

I myself wrote a series on hell for I.V.F.'s <u>His</u> magazine a couple decades ago, but more to the point, published <u>Jonathan Edwards on Heaven and Hell</u> in 1980. Incidentally, the re-publication of Edward Hickman's 2 volume edition of <u>The Works of Jonathan Edwards</u> (1838) by the Banner of Truth in 1974 is, no doubt, the greatest defense of hell (along with all other Christian doctrines) in the twentieth century.

Robert Morey's defense of Orthodoxy, <u>Death and the Afterlife</u> (1984), calls for special mention. It is a more-than-adequate reply to William Fudge's work. I will cite the work from time to time but not nearly as much as it deserves. This is because it operates mainly on the exegetical level and with the definitive lexicons. In a sense, Morey meets Fudge on his own turf with his own weapons, and upsets him so decisively that I wondered that there was a 1985 edition of <u>The Fire That Consumes</u>. I certainly do not agree with Clark Pinnock that Fudge has not been answered. He was devastated centuries before he wrote his book, in fact; but, if anyone confines himself to contemporary

The Conservative Revolt Against Hell

literature, Morey is enough.

The reason I do not cite and quote Morey more is not that he is not persuasively useful, but that he is not necessary for my purpose. In a sense, he mounts a cannon to shoot a fly while I find a fly-swatter sufficient. In fact, I simply take the swatter out of Fudge's hand with which to swat Fudge. In terms of his own material and any rational analysis of it, it collapses under the slightest scrutiny, as I trust the reader can easily see. But if you find more necessary, Morey will more than satisfy. Bryan Allen, while a student at Master's Seminary, sent me a comparison of Fudge and Morey done by Randall Watters of Bethel Ministries, PO Box 3818, Manhattan Beach, CA. If you write Mr. Watters, you may be able to secure a copy.

Very recently, no less a stalwart, orthodox, reformed theologian than Philip Hughes, retired Westminster Theological Seminary (Philadelphia) professor, has come out against hell. Because of Hughes' scholarly stature and conservative reputation, I will examine his statement more closely.

Chapter 37 of Hughes' The True Image is entitled, "Is the Soul Immortal?" (398-407). This chapter begins taking exception to John Calvin's doctrine in Psychopannychia that the soul survives death. Hughes critiques each of the texts Calvin cites to show that the soul is immortal. Since everything rests on the

The Conservative Revolt Against Hell

teaching of the Word of God, let me go over the texts which Calvin cites for, and Hughes against, the immortality of the soul.

First, Calvin cites Matthew 10:28: *"Do not fear those who kill the body but cannot kill the soul, rather fear Him who can destroy both soul and body in hell."* To Calvin, this shows that the soul survives the death of the body. Hughes finds this proving the opposite. It teaches that God "can <u>destroy</u>" the soul in hell. The implication seems clear to Hughes that the soul is not immortal because God can <u>destroy</u> it. But, of course, as Hughes will admit, Calvin did not interpret "destroy" to mean terminate, but torment (eternally). As such, this text is no argument <u>against</u> the immortality of the soul, but a proof of it. Hughes himself is begging the question, simply assuming that Calvin's "destroy" means other than Calvin meant. Fudge will make the same mistake about Christ's meaning, and, when we come to that, I will examine Christ's infallible teaching in Matthew 10:28 more closely.

Here it is sufficient to refute Hughes' attempted refutation of Calvin's interpretation. Christ, in this text, clearly claims that God can do something to men that wicked men cannot do to men. God can kill body <u>and soul</u> while men can kill only the body. But according to the Hughes' interpretation, man also can and does kill body and soul because they are in-

The Conservative Revolt Against Hell

separable. When man kills a man he kills a person, body and soul. God can do no more to man than man can do to man.

Such an inevitable conclusion must embarrass Philip Hughes, who is a theist and believer in the omnipotence of God, to which man's dependent and limited power bears no comparison, not to mention equality. To make the error worse, this very superiority of God's power is what Christ is stressing. To make matters still worse, our Lord is also indicating God's superior power by His ability to destroy body and soul in "hell." But that also is no greater power than man has over man; according to Hughes, God can only annihilate man body and soul and that is precisely what wicked men do when they kill the body. "Hell," for Hughes, is annihilation. If it were, it is within the power of man who, when he kills a fellow-man, kills his soul as well, thus terminating his being.

Hughes next rejects Calvin's appeal to the immortality of the soul in John 2:19: *"Destroy this temple, and in three days I will raise it up,"* which refers, as the Apostle explains, to *"the temple of his body...."* Again, Calvin is right and Hughes is wrong, even according to Hughes' thinking. Calvin was, no doubt, conscious that the reference was to the killing of Christ's body and its resurrection in three days. But, if Christ's body were killed, the soul would no longer be "visible" in

The Conservative Revolt Against Hell

this world; but, would, of course, continue to live; because, after the resurrection of the body, the soul would be with it, as the Apostle John knew had been the case. If the soul had perished with the death of the body, as Hughes assumes, it would have perished permanently because the soul, according to the annihilationists, has no independent existence apart from the body. The body does exist after death as long as its bones remain, but there is no remnant of an immaterial soul. Though the annihilationist says that the soul is inseparable from the body, he cannot say that the body must be inseparable from the soul. All animals have bodies without souls. Our text refers to the resurrection of Christ's body, not His soul which, according to Hughes, must be gone forever since no re-creation of the soul is mentioned in the text. Calvin is right or the human soul of Jesus Christ perished forever.

Luke 23:46 is the next of Calvin's texts cited to prove that the soul of man never dies. Hughes sees no proof in the words of the Lord, *"Father, into thy hands I commit my spirit ...."* (Ps.31:5) David's Psalm 31:5 reads, *"Into thy hand I commit my spirit; thou hast redeemed me, O Lord, faithful God."* Calvin sees the dying Christ committing His spirit to the Father while His body is dying. For Calvin, this means that the soul which Christ commits to God survives the body which is about to die. Hughes seems to infer that if Christ

The Conservative Revolt Against Hell

(and David) had not committed their souls to God, they would have died with their bodies. Certainly this is not stated or necessarily inferred by these words, as Hughes would no doubt grant. He would remind me that he is only saying that Calvin has no right to cite Christ's words as proof that His soul survives the death of His body. But they certainly would so prove. Christ does not pray that His soul survive, but <u>assuming</u> its survival, He commits it to the hands of the Father. David makes the implicit seem even more explicit when he prays for the <u>redemption</u> of his surviving soul by a "faithful God." The same is true of Stephen's dying prayer, "Lord Jesus, receive my spirit (Acts 7:59)," which Calvin uses and Hughes abuses.

Since Dr. Hughes himself says that 1 Pet.3:19 (*"Jesus went and preached to the spirits in prison"*) is one of the most controverted passages in the New Testament, and he does not attempt to refute Calvin's appeal to it, we will let it lie for space's sake. We cannot, however, overlook Ecc.12:7, which surely, even on the <u>surface,</u> justifies Calvin's citation. "The dust returns to the earth as it was, and the spirit returns to God who gave it." The creation surely distinguished between the "dust" of which man's body was made and the soul God "breathed" into it. (Gen.2:7) The one returns to dust and the other to God!

The Conservative Revolt Against Hell

Why does Hughes even question this obvious text? Because, apparently, he has become accustomed to thinking the soul, too, naturally perishes with the body even when the text expressly states that it has a different natural destiny.

A final text of Calvin is "Luke 16:19ff, which speaks of the state after death of the rich man and Lazarus." If any text is more obvious than Ecc.12:7, this would be it. But for Hughes, it is so obviously the opposite of what it obviously is that he finds no comment necessary. So I must endeavor to make the obvious more obvious. Christ's words deal with the rich man and Lazarus after their deaths. That is obvious and unquestioned by anyone. So the souls of these two men, according to Luke 16:19ff, survive death. Why would Hughes and other annihilationists think otherwise? Because the suffering of the rich man especially is represented as bodily (he wants water to alleviate the terrible burning). Therefore, annihilationists reason, the soul is not separated after death from the body. If either exists, they both exist together. There is no separate existence of the soul in hell.

Let me respond. First, this text does prove what Calvin claimed, that the soul does survive death. Second, if the heat and water are to be taken literally, then it would refer to a time of punishment, after death,

The Conservative Revolt Against Hell

when both body and soul are in torment. <u>That, in itself, would not prove that the soul had not existed separately, until a resurrection of the body had taken place</u>. So the passage, any way you take it, does not vouchsafe Hughes' contention that the soul is always inseparable from the body. <u>Third</u>, therefore, the passage is justly cited by Calvin and no way supports the annihilationist position. Indeed, <u>fourth</u>, it is inconsistent with annihilationism inasmuch as it proves punishment of the wicked after death.

After indicating that this early view of Calvin continued throughout his life, Hughes then remarks that "The passages quoted by Calvin indicate that the human soul survives physical death, not that it is <u>in itself</u> immortal" (399, emphasis mine). He continues, "The notion of the <u>inherent immortality</u> of the soul, it is true, has been generally accepted in the Christian church...(emphasis mine)." Dr. Hughes knows that neither Calvin nor the Christian church believed that the soul has any immortality not bestowed on it by its Creator, whatever Plato may have imagined. Only God Himself has "inherent immortality." Dr. Hughes knows this as well as anyone.

Hughes' concern is not really with the <u>inherent</u> immortality of the soul but with <u>any</u> immortality, inherent or bestowed. Why, then, does he not say so? None of all these texts Calvin cited above turn on

The Conservative Revolt Against Hell

<u>inherent</u> immortality, but immortality. And that - immortality - is what Hughes is intent on denying. Why not say so rather than giving the impression that it is the Platonic doctrine of <u>inherent</u> immortality? He suggests that all the Bible is stressing is accountability to God, not life beyond the grave. But accountability to God is not incompatible with life beyond the grave, indeed it requires it because justice is not complete this side of the grave.

Hughes next considers the argument for "inherent" immortality of the soul that man was created in the image of God (400) and rightly refutes it. But that some advocates of immortality of the soul have offered uncompelling arguments is no proof that all its arguments are inconclusive. As Hughes says, immortality of man is "subject to the good pleasure of the Creator." That is exactly the point. It has been, the Bible teaches, the good pleasure of the Creator to create souls that He will <u>never</u> allow to die (even their bodies only die temporarily).

When Dr. Hughes turns from opposing Calvin and the Reformer's sound use of Scripture to the advocacy of his own doctrine, he leaves off opposing truth and takes up the promulgation of positive error. <u>First,</u> he maintains that "man as originally created was both potentially immortal and potential mortal."(400) Man was potentially neither; potentially nothing. In <u>God</u> he

The Conservative Revolt Against Hell

lives, moves, and has his very being. (Acts 17:28) Left to himself, his potentiality was non-existence. He went on existing because the Creator continued to preserve that existence.

<u>Second,</u> a deeper error along the same line follows. Man was created "potentially sinless, but also potentially sinful." Man was made in the image of God which was not "potentially sinless," nor even actually sinless, but positively virtuous. (Col.3:10) Hughes is here unreformed, both in his metaphysics and his anthropology.

<u>Third</u>, in the very same paragraph, the reformed theologian in Philip Hughes almost awakens from its deep sleep as he stresses the image of God and personal fellowship, but can get no further than saying that created man's existence was "quite positively <u>within the sphere</u> of godliness and life" (emphasis mine).

> It was by this rebellion against his Creator that he passed from a positive to a negative relationship and brought the curse upon himself. His death, which is the sum of that curse, is also the evidence that man is not inherently immortal.

Man did not have to sin to prove that he was not "<u>inherently</u> immortal." Being a human creature, good or bad, proved that God would keep him from dying.

The Conservative Revolt Against Hell

Men in heaven, where sin can never enter and where all there will live forever are not "<u>inherently</u> immortal." Only God is inherently immortal. To consider the creature inherently immortal is nothing short of idolatry.

One error leads inevitably, in a logical mind, to another. Now man is seen, <u>fourth</u>, as "<u>integrally compounded</u> of both the spiritual and the bodily." "Man is <u>essentially</u> a corporeal-spiritual entity" (emphasis mine). There is no suggestion that a part of him was undying and therefore that his dying would be in part only." It is more than a "suggestion." It is immediately evident that man's soul died immediately when he first disobeyed God and his body was soon sentenced to pain and suffering. (Gen. 3:11ff, 3:16ff; 1 Tim. 5:6; Eph. 2:1) So Hughes' stress on man's being integrally and essentially a body-soul being is true enough but does not justify his conclusion that the soul cannot survive the body even temporarily. It is, in fact, flatly contradicted in 2 Cor. 5:1-4:

> *For we know that if this earthly tent we live in is destroyed, we have a building from God, a house not made with hands, eternal in the heavens. Here indeed we groan, and long to put on our heavenly dwelling, so that by putting it on we may not be found*

The Conservative Revolt Against Hell

naked. For while we are still in this tent, we sigh with anxiety; not that we would be unclothed, but that we would be further clothed, so that what is mortal may be swallowed up by life.

Jonathan Edwards used this as text for his funeral sermon on the occasion of the death of David Brainerd, in which oration he said: 2 Cor.5:18, "The soul of a saint when it leaves the body at death goes to be with Christ." (p.7) Prepared for Mr. Brainerd's funeral appointed Oct.12, 1747.

Fifth, in the next paragraph (401), Hughes admits that Calvin does not regard the soul as inherently immortal, but in so doing is supposed to be involved in contradiction. How, Hughes asks Calvin, can the soul be immortal only by "the secret inspiration of God," and yet be immortal? Since Calvin is not here, I will dare to answer for him: "It is immortal because God's 'secret inspiration' makes it so, dear Philip, as I have already shown in the texts of Scripture which you so sadly mishandled."

Sixth, after dealing deftly but briefly with a number of classical orthodox texts (402-403) which I will consider in the more extensive similar handlings by William Fudge in following chapters, Hughes, having disposed of John Calvin, takes on Aurelius Augustine

The Conservative Revolt Against Hell

(and Jonathan Edwards with him). He cites Augustine's statement: "What a fond fancy it is to suppose that eternal punishment means long continued punishment, while eternal life means life without end." Hughes grants Augustine's point "so long as it is <u>punishment</u> that is spoken of as being endless." But, he continues, the ultimate contrast "is between everlasting <u>life</u> and everlasting <u>death</u>...." Then Hughes astutely argues that the "notion of death that is everlastingly endured requires the postulation that the damned be kept endlessly alive to endure it" (403).

Before we respond to Hughes' argument, let us stress his concession. He does admit that endless punishment would have to be unending to contrast with unending life. Since this is precisely what Christ says in Matthew 25:46 is the case (the wicked go away to endless punishment), a great annihilationist has granted that that would have to be unending punishment.

Let us return to his point that the parallelism between eternal life and eternal death would imply the termination of death because otherwise an eternal death would have to be an eternal <u>living death</u>, a contradiction in terms. Eternal death would have to be eternal life with which it is being contrasted.

This is a cute argument rather than an acute one. <u>First</u>, if eternal death meant extinction, there would be

The Conservative Revolt Against Hell

nothing eternal about such a death. It would be over once and for all. There would be nothing <u>continuing</u>, much less eternal, about such a death. The expression would self-destruct and convey no meaning. <u>Second</u>, there would be nothing corresponding to and contrasting with eternal life. Hughes and all agree that a parallelism of some sort is intended. This interpretation would leave one meaningful term compared with a meaningless expression. Eternal life we could understand. Eternal death would be a simple contradiction in terms. <u>Third</u>, for any comparison to be meaningful, existence of both elements must be assumed. There are two different kinds of existences, but existence in each case is assumed or no comparison is possible. <u>Fourth</u>, "death" often refers to the termination of one aspect of an existence and not another. Thus, she who <u>lives</u> in pleasure is <u>dead</u> while she lives, I Tim. 5:6. She exists, so far as pleasure is concerned, even though dead in another sense. Likewise, he who loses his life (or dies) gains it (or lives) in another sense, Mark 8:35. "Everlasting death," to be meaningful, must have a dual reference: death in one sense and life in another, and both eternal existences.

So what Dr. Hughes thinks fatal to the Augustinian interpretation of this expression is absolutely inescapable if the statement is not to be reduced to nonsense. But Hughes is not finished yet. He feels that Au-

The Conservative Revolt Against Hell

gustine's case was made hopeless by his belief in literal fire, as if God could not keep a body alive in fire. Our author is beguiled into this obvious error by the fact that Augustine chose to illustrate his point by the salamander that "can live in the fire, in burning without being consumed, in pain without dying." Hughes, having noted that Augustine may have failed in his illustration, quotes Augustine's real point which Hughes imagines to be a retreat. Said Augustine: "Although it is true that in this world there is no flesh which can suffer pain and yet cannot die, yet in the world to come there will be flesh such as there is not now, as there will also be death such as there is not now." Says Hughes: "Augustine, in short, found it necessary to introduce a change in the meaning of <u>death</u> if his belief in the endlessness of the torments of hell fire was to be sustained...." We have already answered this above in Augustine's absence.

<u>Seventh</u>, Hughes is still not finished in his seemingly endless effort to end endless punishment. He has three grand summary concluding arguments merely to state which is enough to expose their futility.

First is a mere repetition of the jejune remark that life is life, death is death, and eternal life is eternal life and eternal death is eternal death. In this one, and really only argument of Dr. Hughes, I gave a four-fold refutation that need not be repeated simply because

The Conservative Revolt Against Hell

this alleged argument is repeated.

Second is the repetition of the true, but already shown to be irrelevant, observation that immortality is not inherent.

Third is Hughes' last desperate attempt to make an end of "endless punishment:" endless punishment is "incompatible" with Christ's redemption. Let me give Hughes' statement, only inserting in brackets what he neglects to mention:

> Christ has appeared once for all at the end of the ages to put away sin by the sacrifice of Himself (Heb.9:26, I Jn.3:5) [for all who accept that sacrifice] that through His appearance death has been abolished (II Tim.1:10), [for all who accept that salvific appearance] and that in the new heaven and the new earth, that is in the whole realm of creation [for the redeemed of the Lord] there will be no more weeping or suffering, 'and death shall be no more,' (Rev.21:4) [for those who believe in Him who is the resurrection and the life]. The conception of the endlessness of the suffering of torment and of the endurance of 'living' death in hell stands in contradiction to this [fallacious] teaching. It leaves a part of creation which, unrenewed, everlastingly exists in alienation from the new heaven and the new earth. It means that suffering and death will never be totally [or at all] removed from the [unredeemed] scene. The inescapable logic of this position was accepted, with shocking [but biblically

The Conservative Revolt Against Hell

faithful] candor, by Augustine who [rightly] affirmed that 'after the resurrection, when the final universal judgment has been completed, there will be two kingdoms, each with its own distinct boundaries, the one Christ's, the other the devil's, the one consisting of good, the other of bad.' To this must be objected that with the restoration of all things in the new heaven and the new earth, which involves God's reconciliation to Himself of <u>all things</u>, whether on earth or in heaven (Acts 3:21, Col.1:20) [which He has actually reconciled], there will be no place for a second kingdom of darkness and death. Where all is light there can be no darkness; for 'the night shall be no more' (Rev.22:5). When Christ fills all in all [salvifically] and God is everything to everyone [who is saved] (Eph.1:23, I Cor.15:28), how is it conceivable that there can be a section or realm of [that] creation that does not belong to this fulness and by its very presence contradicts it? The establishment of God's everlasting kingdom of peace and righteousness will see the setting free of the whole created order [that is redeemed] from bondage to decay as it participates in the glorious liberty of the children of God (Rom.8:21)."
405-406

The fourth argument finds the return of Christ heralding the "death of death." (406) Before I proceed, let me note that Hughes himself here uses death in a way that does not mean death in the ordinary sense. "Death of death" cannot be since death is al-

The Conservative Revolt Against Hell

ready dead unless the second "death" is a <u>living</u> death. Christ at His appearing will destroy death (I Cor. 15:24-26). This is true only for those for whom Christ died and for whom He will return bringing perfect redemption. Hughes answers himself when he cites II Tim. 2:10 saying "without the abolition of death the triumph of life and immortality cannot be complete." But life and immortality is for the redeemed, not for the unredeemed. In them death is destroyed; not for the unredeemed for whom it continues eternally.

This sad chapter of Philip Hughes ends on a "positive" note. It tries to answer the criticism that annihilationism is no punishment at all, much less an adequate punishment, not to mention an eternal punishment. I won't even condescend to quote it. Philip Hughes falls on his own sword, a truly noble but erring friend.

If there is anything sadder than seeing Philip Hughes fall into the terrible error of denying God's eternal punishment of the impenitent wicked, it is seeing the one sometimes called the "pope of the evangelicals," John Stott, do the same.

It is in his response to the more liberal theologian David L. Edwards that Dr. Stott states his views in <u>Evangelical Essentials</u> (InterVarsity Press, 1988). We are here concerned with his response to the liberal

The Conservative Revolt Against Hell

eschatology (306-331). In this area, Stott is not able to give the general evangelical response to the liberal denial of hell, for he himself departs from traditional Orthodoxy. We must, therefore, give an evangelical response to his non-evangelical response.

First, a minor matter in itself, but indicative of a tone, concerns the mere imagery of "fire." Stott observes, truly enough, that fire usually terminates what it burns or consumes. Therefore, he argues, we should anticipate that the "fire" of future judgment should be so anticipated. " Hence it is the smoke (evidence that the fire has done its work) which 'rises for ever and ever, Rev.14:11; cf. 19:3,' " (316). As I said, this is a minor point, but Stott is making a flat reversal of the clear, biblical intention. The smoke of normal fire does not rise "for ever and ever." Smoke goes out when the fire has done its normal work. The whole point of this fire in Revelation is that it has not done its work yet because the smoke continues to rise "<u>for ever and ever</u>." No one just picking up the book of Revelation and reading such language would ever get the impression that this was anything other than a fire that goes on for ever and ever because the smoke it produces rises for ever and ever. One thinks naturally of the word of Christ about a "fire that is <u>not</u> quenched" (Mark 9:48) when one reads of a fire whose smoke ascends for ever and ever.

The Conservative Revolt Against Hell

We are positively amazed when Stott himself turns to these words of Jesus and remarks, "What He says is that the worm will not die and the fire will not be quenched. Nor will they - until presumably their work of destruction is done." Indeed so; which means that their work of destruction never is done because their smoke rises "for ever and ever." Their work is never done because the evidence of its being done is never done.

Stott continues in the same vein openly and seemingly without hesitation wresting what is probably the plainest Scripture of all on this dreadful theme:

> At the end of the so-called parable of the sheep and the goats, Jesus contrasted 'eternal life with 'eternal punishment' (Matthew 25:46). Does this not indicate that in hell people endure eternal punishment? <u>No, that is to read into the text what is not necessarily there.</u> (emphasis mine) What Jesus said is that both the life and the punishment would be eternal, but He did not in the passage define the nature of evil. Because He also spoke of eternal life as a conscious enjoyment of God (John 17:3), it does not follow that eternal punishment must be a conscious experience of pain at the hand of God. On the contrary, although declaring to be eternal, Jesus is <u>contrasting</u> the two destinies: the more unlike they are, the better." (317)

The Conservative Revolt Against Hell

What these two futures have in common is being "eternal;" their contrast is life and punishment which certainly cannot be painless.

Stott's argument is plain:
1. Christ here contrasts <u>eternal</u> life and <u>eternal</u> punishment.
2. Thus, Christ teaches that both future destinies are <u>eternal</u>.
3. Though the <u>duration</u> of the destinies are the same (eternal), their natures (life and punishment) are exactly the opposite.
4. The opposite of life is non-life.
5. Therefore, "eternal punishment" must mean eternal non-existence.

In other words, when Jesus Christ says that the wicked go away into "eternal punishment," He means <u>exactly</u> the opposite: "the wicked go away into eternal non-punishment," according to John Stott. Was there ever a plainer "wresting of Scripture?"

On Dives crying out because he was "in agony in this fire" (Luke 16:23-24,28), Stott sees lost souls realizing "the unimaginably painful realization of their fate. This is not incompatible, however, with their final annihilation" (317-318). So, for Stott hell is momentary at most while the experience of hell is a continuing one in Jesus' account. And, manifestly,

The Conservative Revolt Against Hell

Dives, who begs for a drop of water to relieve his agony just a little would be overjoyed to learn that, being annihilated, he would not suffer anything anymore for ever and ever. Dives longs for a drop of water to afford the slightest relief and even that is refused by Father Abraham. But Father Stott drowns the miserable wretch forever in what, for him, would be showers of blessing.

Having in this manner warded off the doctrine of any future punishment, Stott now marches triumphantly forward under the banner of annihilationism. "Would there not," he asks, "be a serious disproportion between sins consciously committed in time and torment consciously experienced throughout eternity?" (318) But here Stott answers his own objection saying "unless perhaps (as has been argued) the impenitence of the lost also continues throughout eternity." (319) He himself admits the possible ("perhaps") which is to admit the possibility of what he himself considers a legitimate and just explanation of eternal punishment. So John Stott himself cannot say that there cannot be a justifiable ground for eternal torment. Furthermore, Revelation does say that ground will in fact - no "perhaps" - exist. (Rev.22:11)

Also, justice does demand adequate punishment, and Stott himself admits and demands that much. Since punishment itself never produces repentance,

The Conservative Revolt Against Hell

justice requires it to go on forever. Even the very expression, "the annihilation of the wicked," is an outrage against justice, because sin requires punishment, not non-punishment which non-existence certainly is. Stott, though not a universalist, cites universalistic-sounding texts as in some way supportive of the annihilation of the wicked. Since Philip Hughes had dealt with that theme much more extensively and cogently, our remarks where that was considered cover all that is said here and need not be repeated here. Yet I do note Stott's self-contradiction that in the name of justice he faults a just, eternal punishment in favor of a totally unjust non-punishment.

We are glad to include Stott's comment ("I do not dogmatize about the position to which I have come. I hold it tentatively," (320) inadequate as it is. Even that is followed by this unfortunate dogmatism: "I also believe that the ultimate annihilation of the wicked should at least be accepted as a legitimate, biblically-founded alternative to their eternal, conscious torment." As an "alternative," we have a flat rejection and even reversal of the teaching of the Son of God.

Strictly speaking, the next section of the Edwards-Stott dialogue does not deal with hell itself. However, "who will go to hell?" finds Stott incidentally again denying the orthodox, evangelical doctrine of hell. He seems to show, too, that his own unbelief went at least

The Conservative Revolt Against Hell

as far back as 1967. For when he cites the "Congress Statement of Keele 1967: 'A persistent and deliberate rejection of Jesus Christ condemns men to hell.' (I.11), he goes on to mention only that "neither the Lausanne Covenant, nor the Keele Statement which preceded it, said anything about the final destiny of those who had never heard of Christ...."(320) There is no hint here that the "hell" of Keele and Lausanne was not the "hell" of evangelicalism and the Bible.

We evangelicals had generally understood when such statements were made about "hell" they meant "hell," not John Stott's denial of hell. Evangelicals are constantly distressed with liberals taking evangelical terms in an anti-evangelical sense. Here is an evangelical taking evangelical terms in an anti-evangelical sense without apology or explanation. It is inconceivable that John Stott would not know that for the overwhelming majority of evangelicals in 1967 and even 1989 (Lausanne II), "hell" meant eternal punishment and not annihilation, which is what John Stott means by that term.

In this final section of the book, Stott vehemently denies universal salvation. (325) He feels convinced that "the gospel, has not revealed how He (God) will deal with those who have never heard it." (327) Stott personally entertains the hope "that the majority of the human race will be saved." (327) But alas, that gospel

The Conservative Revolt Against Hell

of John Stott's will never save one soul from hell, according to John Stott, for hell does not exist, according to John Stott.

If Edward William Fudge's The Fire That Consumes (1982) was not the start of the current conservative attack on hell, it at least has a central role. The mere blurbs on the book show how broad has been its deleterious influence. F.F.Bruce wrote the foreword. This stalwart Plymouth Brother didn't quite agree with Fudge, nor did he disagree. If one is not for hell as a teaching of the Bible, he must be against it because no one is going to tolerate the teaching of this doctrine if he is not persuaded of its truth. Bruce is misleading when he writes that there is "no unanimity among evangelical Christians" on this theme. Even the present defection by many conservatives has not changed the historic or present overall fidelity to this doctrine. Clark Pinnock testifies that he has seen no answer to Fudge, and infers that he is not the one to refute it. John Wenham finds Fudge making "his main points with force and persuasiveness." Leonard Goss, Editorial Director, Evangelical Book Club, USA, finds Fudge's denial of hell "convincing." No doubt many others have been led astray by this volume who for one reason or another have not published their defection. Being the most formidable defense of "conditional immortality" (better called "modified annihilation-

The Conservative Revolt Against Hell

ism"), Fudge's serious attack on the orthodox doctrine deserves special attention.

CHAPTER 4
EDWARD WILLIAM FUDGE'S PARTICULAR REVOLT

One of the greatest tragedies to befall this century is The Conservative Revolt Against Hell. Hell is the ultimate tragedy. To revolt against its reality is an even greater tragedy because it takes away the warnings that God has graciously given us to avoid the ultimate tragedy of hell. The only thing worse than hell is to deny hell, and that is what Dr. Fudge does.

Edward William Fudge's <u>The Fire That Consumes</u> (1982) is a conditionalist attack on the traditional biblical doctrine of hell. The traditional teaching is that sinners impenitent at death will have their souls sent to hell immediately and later have their resurrected bodies united to their souls, and both punished eternally in hell. The common annihilationist doctrine is that such impenitent sinners are annihilated at death. Between the two, but far closer to annihilationism, is the conditionalist doctrine defended by Dr. Fudge: the impenitent sinner at death is punished in hell according to his degree of guilt and then annihilated, only his ashes remaining in an ever-burning hell.

Our concern here is to show that Fudge's interpretation is incorrect, though I also incidentally critique the annihilationist interpretation as well. If the

Edward William Fudge's Particular Revolt

conditionalists' annihilation after suffering is false, annihilation before any suffering is even more so. Strictly speaking, the conditionalist view is a variety of Annihilationism versus the traditional anti-annihilationist doctrine. The issue is really eternal versus non-eternal suffering. The conditionalist notion of temporary suffering prior to annihilation is virtually nothing compared with eternal suffering, though Fudge will try to make something of it.

Of course, it does involve real pain, but always with the comforting knowledge that some day, relatively soon in contrast to everlasting punishment, it will end. No ray of hope ever comes to comfort those who know that their suffering will never end. Indeed, that is the most awful aspect of such punishment. It will never, ever end, or even be diminished; rather, we shall show, it is likely to be everlastingly increased.

A token punishment versus eternal punishment is the debate between us. I personally could wish the annihilationist could win this debate; but, as I will show in what follows, all such thinking is wishful thinking. If the traditionalists fail in their attempt to end this wishful thinking, the first moment in hell will certainly succeed in extinguishing hope forever.

Little or no future suffering versus eternal suffering is the issue before us. Anyone will admit that, in comparison with this issue, all of the most grave,

Edward William Fudge's Particular Revolt

contemporary problems about which we agonize in newspapers, periodicals, books, T.V., and life every day are trifling. To flee or not to flee from hell is the only really important question. If there be an eternal hell, not to flee while there is time is the ultimate folly.

1. THE WORD "AIONIOS"

After an interesting introductory discussion of the subject of future punishment, <u>The Fire That Consumes</u> takes up its first major argument: the meaning of the New Testament Greek word αιον (*aion*) and its derivatives. The orthodox have traditionally argued that since this word, when associated with "life" is usually translated eternal or everlasting, it must mean the same when associated with death or punishment. Thus they have, Fudge correctly observes, used this word as an argument for eternal punishment and against annihilation. Fudge contends strenuously against this argument.

There is no question that the Greek word *aionios* may, but need not, mean everlasting. All depends on how the biblical text and context use the word (Fudge, 39-40). The word itself means everlasting <u>so far as the thing described is capable of everlastingness</u>. "The sprinkling of blood at the Passover was an 'everlasting' ordinance (Exodus 12:24)." Manifestly, if the

Edward William Fudge's Particular Revolt

Passover ceased, the sprinkling of blood associated with it would cease also. The meaning is that so long as there is a passover there will be the sprinkling of blood. Everlastingness does not lose its meaning because that with which it is associated ceases to be. When the adjective is used, it qualifies the noun, of course. Fudge and the orthodox should agree that in the Bible *aionios* "speaks of unlimited time within the limits determined by the things it modifies."(40) Thus, resurrection to *aionial* life means resurrection to life as long as that resurrection life endures, which, theoretically, could be a microsecond or everlastingly.

At this point, the orthodox have always made an argument which Fudge mentions but does not quite feel. He simply makes the observation above and notes that *aion* does not necessarily mean everlasting, which is admitted by both sides. However, the orthodox are arguing that when *aionial* life and death of human persons are mentioned together in the same context, the word would mean the same thing in each case. All agree that *aionial* life is everlasting. The orthodox argue that *aionial* death in such contexts is everlasting also. It is as infinitely easy for God to preserve human existence in hell everlastingly as to preserve human life in heaven everlastingly. This citing both future existences together certainly does suggest a parallel meaning of *aion*. The burden of

Edward William Fudge's Particular Revolt

disproof is on Fudge. He is crushed under that burden. All he does is irrelevantly point out that in some <u>other</u> contexts the word *aion* does not mean everlasting.

If, therefore, a punishment is said to be *aionic* it lasts as long as its victim lasts. If he ceases, it ceases. If he does not cease, it does not cease. So when our Lord says that the "goats" (evil persons) go away to *aionic* punishment, it means that so long as these evil men exist, their punishment continues. If it can be shown that these sinners do sometime cease to be, so does their punishment. If it cannot be shown, their punishment does not.

Manifestly, the burden of proof lies on those who say that resurrected sinners cease to exist and therefore do not receive unending punishment. The word *aionios* does not require eternal punishment if it can be proved that those sentenced to hell cease in time to exist. Otherwise, the word would mean everlasting punishment.

The <u>content</u> of Matthew 25:46 certainly does not suggest termination of life. The people who heard Jesus say this possibly, or probably, believed that devils, to whose abode wicked men were consigned, were thought to exist forever (though Fudge will challenge this). If humans were sentenced to a place which was to endure forever with their original inhabitants, devils, who were thought to exist forever, presumably

Edward William Fudge's Particular Revolt

they, too, were to exist forever in that place of torment.

There is also a biblical, theological reason to believe that the punishment must be eternal even if the word *aion* were not used at all. If the impenitent sinners were assigned to their own abode, their suffering would be everlasting if God were the Punisher, because He could and would keep the impenitent sinner alive forever because impenitent sinners do not repent in the next world. Punishment never changes people's attitudes. It can change behavior ("scared straight"), when behavior modification terminates the punishment. But God is the Searcher of hearts who is never satisfied with mere outward change, if it is made. So God's punishment would go on forever because the sinner continues to sin and incur God's punishment. Lest God be mocked, whatever a man sows, that he must reap as long as he sows, which is forever and forever.

Fudge has a lengthy discussion of man's natural immortality of soul and rejects that "Platonic" doctrine which he thinks is unbiblical. Indeed, the argument is humorous because man is not even naturally "mortal," not to mention immortal, for he depends on God every moment for any existence. Whether man's soul is naturally immortal or not, it will be immortal if God chooses to keep it from dying. Fudge will never deny that God can do this to those in hell (though

Edward William Fudge's Particular Revolt

Fudge is confident that God <u>will</u> do it for those in heaven), but he thinks God <u>will not</u> do it. God, Fudge admits, punishes sinners in hell. We say against Fudge, that the punishment must then go on forever because neither God nor the sinner ever changes. This is where Fudge's temporary punishment is a fatal disadvantage from which strict annihilationists do not suffer. If God annihilates a sinner, unjust as that would be, it would terminate the sinner. Fudge's sinner can never be terminated by a holy God because he goes on sinning and must go on being punished by a holy God who will never clear the guilty, Ex.34:7.

In any case, the natural immortality of the soul question is irrelevant here. God can make it and the body immortal if He chooses, everyone admits. The only question is whether He does so choose. I have shown that a holy and just God must make the sinner's body and soul immortal in order that he receive his deserved punishment. If the sinner died, God's justice would die with him. Anyone, therefore, who admits that God is holy, just, and omnipotent logically admits that the punishment of evil persons will be everlasting.

The passage in question implies that God <u>does</u> eternally punish. These sinners are sentenced to *aionic* punishment by the divine Judge who is able to continue their existence forever and, therefore, does because He remains God and they remain impenitent

Edward William Fudge's Particular Revolt

sinners. *Aionic*, it is agreed, means duration as long as that with which or whom the word is associated. Here it is associated with those whom the divine Judge sentences to a punishment which, in the nature of the case, must be everlasting, never-ending punishment. *Aionic* means everlasting if it can mean everlasting, and here it must, especially when compared with <u>*aionic* life</u>. Notice that *aionic* does not prove that the punishment is eternal, but the fact that the punishment is eternal is what proves that *aionic* , which, linguistically speaking, <u>may</u> mean everlasting, here <u>must</u> mean everlasting.

Furthermore, the sinners' bodies are visibly present, therefore raised from the dead. This also implies eternal punishment. Their bodies had died, but they are raised again for one purpose, punishment. This is for sins done in the flesh, Rom.8:3. The body is merely an instrument of the soul and not the source of sin. Yet it is being punished along with the soul. We have shown that the soul's punishment must be eternal. If the body, as the instrument of the soul's sinning, is to be punished along with the soul and the soul's punishment is eternal, the punishment of the body must be for the same eternal period. Not only does God preserve the soul immortal but the body also, which is something that Plato did not apparently envisage. So the Bible, which Fudge wants to distance from Plato,

Edward William Fudge's Particular Revolt

is out-Platoing Plato.

We have seen that the fact that God is punishing the sinner shows that the punishment must be everlasting. God is everlasting and the sin of man for which he is being punished lasts forever. Sinners exist forever to be punished forever. We have noted that punishment does not change sinners. It does make them <u>more</u> sinful. Resenting divine punishment is an added sin. The more sin, the more punishment. The more punishment, the more sinfulness, endlessly.

Increase in sinfulness and punishment is conjectural. However, everything implies it and nothing prevents it. That is, these unchanged sinners who hate God will hate and curse God for the punishing. That certainly increases their sin and incurs more punishment. Their guilt, in other words, is constantly increased and so their deserved punishment. Nothing implies this increase will ever cease because God can and, as a just and holy God, must continue being a just and holy God who will, as He can, continue punishing according to the degree of guilt.

Fudge himself claims that sinners will be punished in hell <u>according to their guilt</u>. He does not notice that that implies eternal punishment. He is arguing for eternal punishment without realizing it.

If a sinner is going to be punished one minute in hell, he is going to be punished forever. All agree

Edward William Fudge's Particular Revolt

that there is no repentance but only resentment in the wicked after death, Rev.22:11. Resentment, hatred, cursing, and no repentance ever means that sinners keep earning the wages of sin forever - and receiving them forever. The sinner dies forever or God, the righteous Judge who will not clear the guilty, dies forever.

The punishment does not change and cannot change because the sinner does not change into another kind of being. In this world, there is hope that he may. In the next world, there is no possibility. "Now" is the day of salvation, Ps.95:7; Heb.3:7,13,15; 4:7. "Then" is the day of damnation.

Fallen man is not only wicked in his behavior but in his very nature. His behavior could be modified in this world by punishment, but never his nature. In this world there is some benefit in "behavior modification." I remember Martin Luther King, Jr. saying in a sermon that "you can't legislate morality. Laws can't keep people from hating me but it can keep them from killing me." That was true for a long time before he was murdered. Where God, who searches the heart, is the Punisher, hypocritical behavior modification would accomplish nothing. It would not, therefore, happen. When there is no benefit from not cursing God with their lips so long as they continue to curse Him in their hearts, sinners in hell will curse God inwardly and

Edward William Fudge's Particular Revolt

outwardly in that eternal stench-hole, whose only excuse for existence must be the glorification of God's holiness, justice, and omnipotent power, Rom.9:18,22.

There is no question that *aionios* sometimes signifies quality of existence as it usually does in the expression "<u>eternal</u> life," where the life is a blessed, eternal life. Fudge makes much of this undisputed fact which is irrelevant to the issue of whether *aionios* means unending duration. It is granted that any existence of rational beings will have some quality, happiness or unhappiness. As a quality, this says nothing, of itself, about the duration of the happiness or unhappiness. At any rate, I have shown that hell proves *aionios* means eternal rather than *aionios* proving hell eternal.

Dr. Fudge and others slip into the error of making quality a substitute for everlastingness rather than a mere qualification of the type of existence, whatever its duration. Thus, "based on this Jewish eschatological usage, <u>aionios</u> sometimes suggests quality of being, almost meaning 'divine' <u>rather than</u> 'enduring.'" (41) On the next page, our author cites Donald Bloesch's observation that in the New Testament use of "eternal life," the adjective <u>aionios</u> refers to "the quality <u>more than</u> to the length of life."(emphasis mine) This is possible, but stress on the quality of life implies nothing about its duration.

Edward William Fudge's Particular Revolt

So far from anything being "divine" rather than "enduring," its being "divine" even suggests that it must be endlessly enduring as I have shown. It is virtually redundant to speak of enduring divinity. There is no other kind of divinity. But it must be remembered that the everlasting punishment is a divine sentence as much as the eternal life. If one <u>aion</u> is eternal, it would seem that the other is also. "Behold then the kindness and severity of God...." (Rom.11:22)

It is agreed that the impenitent are punished as long as they continue to exist. It is also agreed that the word <u>aion</u> does not, in itself, determine the duration of the impenitent. The same would be admitted of <u>aion</u> in relation to "life;" <u>it</u> does not determine the duration of the penitent. It is also agreed that the word <u>aion</u> would likely have the same duration meaning for impenitent and penitent. The everlastingness of life for the penitent would be determined by the infinite value of Christ's redemption. This, then, <u>first</u> suggests everlastingness for the punishment of the impenitent. A <u>second</u> argument for the everlastingness of punishment is that the impenitent remain sinful still, Rev.22:11, and so must be unendingly punished. <u>Third</u>, if the heinousness of sin is relative to the dignity of the person against whom it is committed, it is infinite and must be punished infinitely (everlastingly). Moreover, <u>fourth</u>, that the place of this punishment, according to

Edward William Fudge's Particular Revolt

Jesus Christ, is gehenna (the place of unending fire and worms), also spells everlasting punishment. Thus the word <u>allows</u> the meaning everlasting (punishment) and the biblical context demands it.

Fudge does agree on "the endlessness of the bliss," p.42, but that is not because of the use of the word *aionios*. There is nothing wrong with his argument here because eternality can be and is indicated by other items in a context than the word *aionios*. I have admitted that the <u>mere use</u> of that word does not prove that what it modifies is literally everlasting. But the contexts of "life" and "punishment" show it to mean everlasting in both cases, though the quality of those external existences be perfectly lovely in one instance and perfectly vile in the other.

Incidentally, Morey argued the same point on the basis of language. "To say that <u>aion</u> only means 'pertaining to the coming age' is not enough. It has been pointed out by many scholars that when <u>aion</u> refers to the final order it means 'pertaining to the endless age to come'" (<u>Death and the Afterlife</u>, p.129). I may add that Morey has a fine discussion of <u>olam</u> and <u>aion</u> citing Brown, Driver, and Briggs; Girdlestone and others (pp.112-114). This specifically may be mentioned:

Edward William Fudge's Particular Revolt

> Understanding removes one of the arguments used by the annihilationists. They have argued that everlasting punishment does not mean everlasting punishment because the word "everlasting" is used of mountains in Hab.3:6 (KJV). Therefore they argue that the punishment will only be temporal and not eternal.
>
> What the annihilationists fail to realize is that they are ignoring the relative contexts of olam. When it is used to speak of such things as mountains, it has reference to things which exist throughout different generations in this present world. When olam is used of the final order of things, it always means endlessness in the fullest sense. The respective context for olam should not be ignored.

2. Hebrews 6:2

Fudge considers the text Heb.6:2, which refers to the "resurrection of the dead and eternal judgment." Strangely, he remarks: "Once the judging is over, the judgment will remain. The eternal everlasting issue of the once-for-all process of judgment." One can see here that Fudge is tripping over his own language. "Judgment" means condemnation, punishment, not mere verdict. The verdict, that the Judge finds the man guilty, is once for all and finished, everlastingly finished, to be sure. That is true of every verdict that ever has been or shall be rendered. It is then past, forever

Edward William Fudge's Particular Revolt

past. That that is what the writer of Hebrews means by "eternal judgment" is unbelievable. Every judgment is an "eternal judgment" in that sense, and obviously so. "The eternal, everlasting issue of the once-for-all process of judgment" is that "the judgment will remain"! What an issue - that the judgment once made remains once made! Once a verdict, it always remains the verdict then rendered. The consequence of anything ever done is that it everlastingly remains then once done. That doesn't even tell us what the verdict was, but simply that once given it ever remains that once-given verdict. Heb.6:2 was an "eternal judgment," that is, a condemnation, a damnation, a punishment eternally in effect and not simply a once-for-all-given verdict as all other verdicts, whatever they may have been.

Innocuous as this reductionism of Fudge may be here, it is the essential error of his whole book and position. For him, that the fire consumes once for all <u>is</u> the fire that <u>eternally</u> consumes! If the subject were not so serious, and Fudge himself so serious, one would swear he was joking. However serious he may be, trivialization of eternal judgment is one massive crime. Fudge makes "eternal judgment" into no judgment at all, but merely a verdict which stands forever without punishment though, coincidentally, Fudge does say that there will be a little actual punishment.

Edward William Fudge's Particular Revolt

I realize that Fudge is <u>thinking</u> of the issue being the <u>consequence</u> of punishment (annihilation), which is all that is everlasting, in his opinion. What he speaks of, however, is an everlasting issue of that <u>judgment</u>. How could it be an "everlasting issue" if it ended in time? Fudge will say that <u>is</u> the consequence of that judgment (termination of life) and that termination is forever.

To put it more simply: if something is an "eternal judgment," it is not an "eternal issue" of the judgment. A judgment is one thing, an issue of it is another. The issue for Fudge of this "judgment" is annihilation, which is not an "eternal," but a temporal <u>judgment</u>, if any judgment. It is the consequence of a temporal judgment which itself issues in non-entity. It is meaningless to say a non-entity is an "eternal judgment." To be made a non-entity is not even a temporal judgment. A non-entity is nothing. It does not exist in eternity or time. It is nothing. Certainly it is not judgment.

Those who favor annihilation of the wicked at death have one problem, and those, like Fudge, who favor annihilation after temporal punishment have another problem. The pure annihilationists have the problem with the noun because there is no punishment, since annihilation is <u>no</u> punishment of a being but the extinction of being. The conditional annihila-

Edward William Fudge's Particular Revolt

tionists have a problem with the adjective because there is no eternal punishment. Passovers and mountains may cease to exist, but human beings do not necessarily cease to exist. They can be kept alive eternally, as they are temporally, in Him in whom we live and move and have our being, Acts 17:28. If Heb.6:2 says that this is an "eternal judgment," then the once-for-all judged are to be kept alive eternally to receive this judgment. The judgment is once for all, but the execution of the once-for-all-given judgment must be eternal.

3. Mark 3:29

Fudge's discussion of the "eternal sin" is quite incorrect, but instead of proving that criticism let me attempt to show that Christ's expression must mean an eternal sin that involves an eternal punishment - which Dr. Fudge tries to show it does not mean. Of course, the expression cannot literally refer to this sin's being eternally committed. It is an eternal sin, not eternal sinning that is in view. All that a temporal creature does is a temporal not eternal act, even if it goes on everlastingly. The sin's being eternal seems to mean that it stands eternally, is irrevocable, irremovable, because Christ indicates that it will never be forgiven, as any other sin could be forgiven in this world,

Edward William Fudge's Particular Revolt

(Cf.Matt.12:32). Now if any sin is eternally unforgivable it must be eternally on the record. And a sin which eternally remains on the record, eternally unforgivable, must be eternally punished if God is eternally just.

To be sure, Orthodoxy finds the Bible to teach that <u>all unrepented</u> sins are eternal in that sense. This sin differs in that it is <u>unrepentable</u> even in this world, therefore unrepentable anywhere. It is therefore eternally unforgivable. Eternally unforgiven sin must be punished eternally. Sin must be forgiven or punished. This sin cannot ever be forgiven, so it must ever be punished. More strictly speaking, all sin must be punished in Jesus Christ or in the sinner himself. This sin will never be punished in Jesus Christ and must therefore be punished in the sinner, OR GOD IS NOT A HOLY AND JUST GOD.

Fudge concludes his paragraph: "This 'eternal' sin was committed once. But its result remains for eternity." (46) Once again Fudge is changing the text. The text says "eternal sin." Fudge renders it eternal "result." An eternal result is not an eternal sin. Furthermore, this sin being "eternal" or forever unforgivable must be forever punished. Fudge's statement that this sin's "result remains for eternity" is true in a way he never sees. The "result" that "remains for eternity" for an eternally unforgivable sin must be its proper

Edward William Fudge's Particular Revolt

wages, eternal punishment. Extinction of the person is extinction of the sin, not any punishment of it.

Fudge does not see this because he correctly observes that this sin was committed only once and in time. It is not being committed eternally, in the view of the text. I have to insert "in the view of the text" because the text is not focusing on this aspect of the matter, though it is true that the sin is unrepented, because unforgiven, and therefore eternally renewed. From this, Fudge wrongly concludes in the face of the text that it is not an "eternal sin" which he further wrongly reduces to an "eternal consequence." But Scripture says it is an "eternal sin" and so it is, because it is never removed or cancelled or erased. Since God must give sins what they deserve, an "eternal sin" must receive eternal punishment; but the sin and its result are still two different things, a simple observation that Dr. Fudge never observes.

Fudge's handling of Heb.9:12 provides a good example of his bad thinking. He observes that Heb.9:12 represents Christ as obtaining "eternal redemption" by appearing "once for all at the end of the ages to do away with sin by the sacrifice of Himself (9:25-26). But this once-for-all act or redeeming, which is finished will never be repeated and can never be duplicated, issues in a redemption which will never pass away. 'Eternal' speaks here again of the <u>result</u> of the

Edward William Fudge's Particular Revolt

action, not the act itself. Once the redeeming has taken place, the redemption remains." (45)

This is linguistically parallel, Fudge thinks, to the wicked being punished once-for-all and the effect of it being non-existence ever after. My reply:

1. It is true that Christ was punished for His people once-for-all and they, as a result have eternal life.
2. That was because Christ is a divine person and His once suffering vicariously has infinite value.
3. Therefore Christ's death merits eternal life for those for whom He died.
4. At the Day of Judgment, the wicked is once-for-all given a sentence of everlasting punishment.
5. If the wicked person was then annihilated he would have received no punishment.
6. Since he is to receive everlasting punishment, he must be kept alive everlastingly to receive everlasting punishment.
7. The sinner's receiving his first punishment could not be once-for-all because he is not a divine person who can receive an infinite (everlasting) punishment in a moment as could the divine Jesus Christ.

Edward William Fudge's Particular Revolt

8. So his punishment would have to go on everlastingly to fulfill the sentence. If he were annihilated, he would never receive everlasting punishment.
9. This would stand even if a person would question (as some orthodox do), whether the wicked under punishment everlastingly resent it and therefore incur it everlastingly, even increasingly so.
10. Fudge appears to have overlooked the difference between a divine Person suffering and a finite human sinner suffering
11. Fudge may be tempted to reply that "Gerstner misses my whole point which was strictly linguistic. I showed that Heb.9:12 is an illustration of the fact that a once-for-all punishing could have an everlasting effect."

I get and admit his point that a once-for-all punishing can bring an eternal or everlasting effect, redemption (glorious life) or punishment (annihilation of life). But my point is that the sinner's once-for-all punishment, unlike the divine Christ's once-for-all punishment, having no such infinite value, could not equal the everlasting punishment they deserve and which must, therefore, be undergone everlastingly by them

Edward William Fudge's Particular Revolt

who have no divine substitute.

12. Incidentally, one sees the dreadful demeaning of the cross of Christ by Fudge's exposition:

   (1) According to Annihilationism, the wicked only deserve to be annihilated.
   (2) Therefore, in its view, they would earn annihilation.
   (3) Christ's death for His sinful people, therefore, would only bring them back from annihilation, affecting a <u>re-creation</u> rather than a <u>redemption</u>.
   (4) In that case, Christ would have died in vain (unnecessarily). Re-creation from non-being would not require the shedding of the blood of the Son of God who then was crucified on the cross for nothing at all.
   (5) Our Lord and Savior, in whose cross we once gloried, we would have to recognize as the ultimate man from La Mancha, except that tilting at windmills would, by comparison to our divine Ideal, appear sheer sobriety.
   (6) To make matters still worse, God the Father so loved the world that He sent His

only Son on such an errand and the Third Person of the Trinity collaborated thoroughly in this divine farce.

(7) Our praises would stick in our throat eternally.

4. <u>2 Thessalonians 1:9</u>

Fudge interprets: "They will be punished with everlasting destruction and shut out from the presence of the Lord and from the majesty of His power," (2 Thess.1:9) as meaning that sinners being punished with an everlasting annihilation will be shut out of the presence and majesty of the Lord's power. Once again, if one did not feel otherwise from reading this book and the solemnity of this theme, one could not believe Fudge is serious.

Fudge tries to give weight to this exegesis by observing that this everlasting destruction and being shut out from the presence and majesty of the Lord happens on the day Christ returns (v.10). "It will not be happening forever, but when He has brought about their destruction, its results will never end." (47) Fudge simply overlooks the words "punished" and "shut out" which signify suffering and not mere deprivation. Annihilation is what sinners want - to be put out of their misery. Eat, drink, be merry, and die. What could

Edward William Fudge's Particular Revolt

be nicer? No karma, no judgment, no punishment. Mere extinction. The wages of sin, according to Fudge, is nothingness and being shut out from something which non-being could never miss. Being "shut out from the presence of the Lord and from the majesty of His power" when people are extinct is no deprivation.

Nothing can't "miss" anything. It is sillier than saying that rocks are "shut out from the presence of the Lord" for they, though they are also incapable of apprehending the presence of the Lord, at least do exist.

Unlike pure annihilationists (whose position Fudge's words here imply, because "destruction" is interpreted as annihilation), he does require some punishment of the wicked. "This retribution ('destruction') will be preceded by penal suffering exactly suited to each one's degree of guilt by a holy and just God...."

We have already shown how right that statement is and that it spells eternal punishment. However, Fudge concludes his sentence:

> ...but that penal suffering <u>within itself</u> is not the ultimate retribution or punishment. There will be an act of destroy<u>ing</u>, resulting in a destruct<u>ion</u> that will never end or be reversed. The act of destroying includes penal pains, but they will end. The result of destruction will

Edward William Fudge's Particular Revolt

never be reversed and will never have an end" (47).

The reader can surely see the absurdity of this interpretation, but let me point it out nevertheless. <u>First</u>, this interpretation represents God as unjust because the "penal suffering <u>within itself</u> is not the ultimate retribution or punishment." Fudge is saying that the punishment sinners do receive is not ultimate retribution or punishment. Yet that temporal punishment is all that they do receive, according to Fudge's interpretation, inasmuch as annihilation is no retribution or punishment, but mere termination of being. Therefore, <u>second</u>, the "destroy<u>ing</u> resulting in a destruc<u>tion</u> that will never end..." makes God still more unjust inasmuch as He is represented as terminating punishment before it is adequate punishment. The sinner never, according to Fudge's interpretation of 2 Thess.1:9, receives just punishment for his sins and this the Word of God could never imply or say, unless the Judge of heaven and earth can do wrong. "Is God unjust, humanly speaking, to inflict His wrath? Of course not!" (Rom.3:6)

Fudge says that "the act of destroying includes penal pains...." Certainly the <u>word</u> "destruction" in English or Greek does not necessarily include the idea of pain, not to mention penal pain. Certainly God

Edward William Fudge's Particular Revolt

could destroy every living creature in a time so small, or no time, that no one would feel anything.

I must keep repeating that annihilation is an alternative to or substitute for pain, not a form of it. People in misery beg for annihilation as the cessation of pain. Fudge himself recognizes this, which is the reason he avoids the usual annihilationist doctrine. But, as I say, "conditionalism" is rejected by the orthodox and the consistent unorthodox alike. The question is: punishment or no punishment. If there is to be punishment, all agree that it must be just or adequate punishment. As shown, the only just punishment for sinners is everlasting punishment. Inadequate or unjust punishment is worse than none because it represents God as not only unjust, but as halting between two opinions. To be wholly just or wholly unjust would be the question for the conditionalists' ever vacillating, ever unstable, ever miserable deity.

True annihilationists recognize this, but Fudge's conservativism calls for some punishment prior to annihilation, and thus he is driven to insert that in the text which is not there in the place Fudge puts it. Denuded of that, "eternal destruction" must mean "eternal annihilation," which redundancy even sounds absurd, but not quite so absurd as "eternal annihilation after a period of suffering" as the meaning of "eternal destruction." If the text meant to say eternal destruction after some punishment it could simply say: "after punishment, the Lord annihilated His enemies." No one needs to be told that annihilated sinners are gone forever, not punished forever.

Even God could not raise them again, because God can't raise what is not there to raise. If the text meant to say what Mr. Fudge would have it say, all that is necessary is: "the Lord will punish the wicked and then destroy them without letting them ever enjoy His presence or divine majesty." But eternal destruction is endless dying aggravated all the more by never enjoying the presence of the Lord and His majesty, as the damned, no doubt, know that the holy angels and redeemed mankind do.

5. Matthew 25:46

I print the whole parable of the sheep and the goats because it is the fullest account in the whole Bible of the Day of Judgment. Let us have it all before us as we consider Fudge's interpretation.

> 31. But when the Son of Man comes in His glory, and all the angels with Him, then He will sit on His glorious throne.
> 32. And all the nations will be gathered before Him; and He will separate them from one another, as the shepherd separates the sheep from

Edward William Fudge's Particular Revolt

the goats;
33. and He will put the sheep on His right, and the goats on the left.
34. Then the King will say to those on His right, "Come, you who are blessed of My Father, inherit the kingdom prepared for you from the foundation of the world.
35. For I was hungry, and you gave Me something to eat; I was thirsty and you gave Me drink; I was a stranger, and you invited Me in.
36. naked, and you clothed Me; I was sick, and you visited Me; I was in prison, and you came to Me."
37. Then the righteous will answer Him, saying, "Lord, when did we see You hungry, and feed You, or thirsty, and give You drink?
38. And when did we see You a stranger and invite You in, or naked, and clothed You?
39. And when did we see You sick, or in prison, and come to You?"
40. And the King will answer and say to them, "Truly I say to you, to the extent that you did it to one of these brothers of Mine, *even* the least *of them*, you did it to Me."
41. Then He will also say to those on His left, "Depart from Me, accursed ones, to the eternal fire which has been prepared for the devil and his angels;
42. for I was hungry, and you gave Me *nothing* to eat; I was thirsty, and you gave Me nothing to drink.

Edward William Fudge's Particular Revolt

43. I was a stranger, and you did not invite Me in; naked, and you did not clothe Me; sick and in prison, and you did not visit Me."
44. Then they themselves will also answer, saying, "Lord, when did we see You hungry, or thirsty, or a stranger, or naked, or sick, or in prison, and did not take care of You?"
45. Then He will answer them, saying, "Truly I say to you, to the extent that you did not do it to one of the least of these, you did not do it to Me."
46. And these will go away into eternal punishment, but the righteous into eternal life.

Fudge:

> ... the life and punishment of this passage are never to end. They are 'eternal' in the sense of <u>everlasting</u>. But we need to note...that 'punishment' is an act or process .... The act or process happens in a fixed period of time but is followed by a result that lasts forever. In keeping with that Scriptural usage, we suggest that the 'punishment' here includes whatever penal suffering God justly issues to each person but consists primarily of the total abolition and extinction of the person forever. The punishing continues until the process is completed and then it stops. But the punishment which results will remain forever. (p.48)

Take that last sentence: "But the punishment which

Edward William Fudge's Particular Revolt

results will last forever." Fudge himself uses the lan-language "punishment which results," which is a contradiction of his labored exegesis. He insisted that it is the <u>effect</u> of the punishing (the abolition of the person), that lasts forever. But here it is the "punishment" of the person which results. A non-existent, annihilated person cannot suffer punishment. Only a living person can undergo punishment, and Christ says it is "eternal punishment." I am being trifling here, but it is only to show that the Conditionalist cannot even state his error without self-contradiction.

This passage of our Lord being the fullest biblical exposition of the Last Judgment, makes Fudge's gross misrepresentation the nadir of his whole book. The clearer Christ's teaching shines here, the more hopelessly obfuscating Dr. Fudge's exposition is seen to be.

After a general description of the scene, Fudge writes that "punishment is an act or process." To be sure, punishment can be either an act or a process. Here a process is implied when Christ says that the wicked go away to "everlasting punishment." Even their "going away" is a process and not one act, and they are going away to "everlasting punishment" which cannot be one act or a limited process. According to Fudge, "the act or process happens in a fixed period of time," which is a flat contradiction of his

Edward William Fudge's Particular Revolt

Lord who says it is "<u>eternal</u> punishment."

Dr. Fudge does not mean to contradict his Lord Jesus Christ. He thinks he avoids it by distinguishing between the punishment and its duration; between the "eternal" and the "punishment." However, what Christ has joined together Fudge rends asunder. He says, arbitrarily, that the punishment "happens in a fixed period of time," though Christ says it is "everlasting." Of course, he tries to distinguish punishing from punishment. But in this judgment scene, Christ declares the wicked cursed and sentenced to "eternal fire," (v.41), and then says (v.46) *These will go away into eternal punishment*. The cursing is not the punishment but the prelude to that which is the "eternal punishment."

Again, Fudge says that "everlasting" does not refer to punishment to which his Lord refers it. Fudge refers it to the <u>result</u> of punishment which is "total abolition and extinction of the person forever," whereas Jesus says that the <u>wicked</u> go away to <u>everlasting punishment</u>, which cannot conceivably be "total abolition and extinction" which, so far from being <u>everlasting</u> punishment, is <u>no</u> punishment. The contrast is absolute. Jesus Christ says that the wicked go away to everlasting punishment and Edward William Fudge says they go away to extinction.

Christ says "everlasting punishment." Fudge says "everlasting result of punishment." These are two

Edward William Fudge's Particular Revolt

drastically different statements. Christ is saying one thing and Fudge another. And the other thing Fudge is saying is not only another, but an absolutely contradicting other. Fudge is rejecting Christ to His face, all the while intending reverence and faithfulness. Christ says that the wicked go away to everlasting punishment. Fudge says, "Not so, Lord, it is only the effect of their punishment that they go away into. Their punishment is only for a relative moment. It is the <u>effect</u> that is eternal."

So utter is this error that if it were the only error in the book it would vitiate it entirely. When any man, not to mention a Christian man, contradicts the Lord to His face, I can see no hope for that man short of condign repentance while there is time.

Suppose, for example, the "eternal punishment" for putting a man's eye out were having one's own eye put out. That would be called an "eternal punishment" because it would be a once-for-all punishing and an eternal punish<u>ment</u>. That is, the punishment would last forever. The person would be forever without that eye. He may use a false eye, get another eye by transplanting, or even have his own gouged eye repaired and replaced. But that <u>original eye as it was originally in his head</u> is gone forever. That, according to Fudge, would be eternal punish<u>ment</u>. The state could even rule that that eye must be destroyed so

Edward William Fudge's Particular Revolt

that it cease eternally ever to exist in its original socket.

Can anyone seriously imagine that that is what Heb. 6:2 means by "eternal punishment?" Suppose the punishment for plucking out a neighbor's one hair was to be punished by having one hair of one's own head pulled out and burned in an oven, that would be eternal punishment. That criminal would have suffered <u>eternal</u> punishment. Serious themes cannot be easily trivialized. Nevertheless, Conditionalists succeed without trying because having eternal punishment equated with annihilation is the greatest trivialization of eternal punishment. As I must keep repeating, annihilation is <u>no</u> punish<u>ment</u>, even punish<u>ing</u>, if done by God as is assumed in the Bible. God can certainly practice painless annihilation with an efficiency the state can never perfectly achieve even with the removal of a hair.

Christ would be saying that the "goats" go away to non-existence. After citing all their crimes, He tells those on His left side, "Go away to a place where you will never suffer again. Any punishment you will ever suffer you have already suffered. The only hell there is is in the world from which I am now eternally delivering you, this present world."

Whatever time is taken in the "goats" "going away," would surely be used up in rejoicing. "This,"

Edward William Fudge's Particular Revolt

the wicked would shout, "is better than our own request of having the mountains fall on us!" If they were capable of it, they would even be tempted to thank and praise God, before blessed oblivion.

CHAPTER 5

FUDGE ON THE OLD TESTAMENT

In "The Soul is Immortal, But... (The Philosophers versus the Fathers)," p.65, Fudge argues that there is no biblical teaching that the human soul is an indestructible being, by its very nature. He is aware that the Creator **may** continue the soul after death, but does not seem to realize that he, Fudge, must prove that the Bible says God **will not** preserve the soul eternally if his chapter is to militate against eternal punishment. The chapter is instructive and interesting, but irrelevant to the argument because, even if it proved that the soul is not <u>naturally</u> immortal, it does not prove that God will not preserve it forever. Even if it were naturally mortal that does not prove that its punishment would not be immortal or eternal.

W.G.T.Shedd and some other traditionalists correctly maintain that Sheol sometimes is the word for hell in the Old Testament. The majority of contemporary biblical scholars are opposed. Even orthodox Harry Buis, citing Oehler, says that in the Old Testament, "good and evil continue to exist together after death."(82) I think this is an error, but I am here concerned with Fudge who draws this conclusion:

Fudge on the Old Testament

> Anyone with a concordance can verify these statements for himself. Faithful Jacob expected to go "down to Sheol" when he died (Gen.37:35 ; 42:38; 44:29,31). Righteous Job longed to hide in Sheol until God's anger passed him by (Job 14:13). David, the man after God's heart, viewed Sheol as his resting place, though he trusted God to redeem him from its grasp (Ps.49:15). Even Jesus Christ, the Holy one of God, went to Sheol (Greek: hades) upon His death (Ps.16:10, Acts2:24-31). There is simply no basis for making Sheol an exclusive place of punishment for the wicked. (82)

I know of no one who makes Sheol mean hell <u>exclusively</u>. Even Fudge himself goes on to show that Sheol is translated by the King James as "hell" (31 times), "the grave" (31 times), or "the pit" (3 times). The American Standard version left it "Sheol." The NIV usually makes it "grave" and LeRoy Froom, "gravedom."

One can see from this data what the translators are doing. All see Sheol as a common end to this present life for the righteous and the wicked. The ASV simply leaves the word Sheol standing as the terminus of human life in this world; the NIV and Froom give the English vernacular for that which is "grave" or "gravedom;" and the KJV, drawing on contexts, finds that "grave" or "pit" is all that is signified some 34 times while in 31 instances judgment is associated

Fudge on the Old Testament

with wicked persons going to Sheol and that judgment associated with death, spells "hell" in the Bible.

If one consults the concordance he will see that Sheol is indeed associated with judgment in many cases, though not all. If one sees that the Bible teaches that the wicked's condemnation at death incurs hell, he is compelled to conclude that is indeed the meaning of Sheol in such passages. Thus we have, from that word "Sheol" alone, 31 or so Old Testament teachings of the doctrine of eternal damnation.

Furthermore, though this goes beyond the domain of translation, if Sheol applied to the wicked means hell, then all references to Sheol mean hell so far as the wicked are concerned. Likewise, though we are not now discussing that theme, if the Bible teaches that death for the righteous means "heaven," every Old Testament occurrence of Sheol spells an Old Testament teaching of an eternal heaven so far as the "righteous" are concerned. The New Testament would be bringing all this to far greater "light" somewhat as an electric light outshines a candle. But what is "patent" in the New Testament is, as Augustine declared, at least "latent" in the Old Testament. This doctrine is patent enough in the Old Testament and only more patent in the New.

Calvin's survey of "the agreements of the Testaments on eternal life" is so classic I must quote his

Fudge on the Old Testament

summary (Institutes, II, XI, 23):

> There are two remaining points: that the Old Testament fathers (1) had Christ as pledge of their covenant, and (2) put in him all trust of future blessedness. These I shall not labor to prove because they are less controversial and clearer. Let us, therefore, boldly establish a principle unassailable by any stratagems of the devil: the Old Testament or Covenant that the Lord had made with the Israelites had not been limited to earthly things, but contained a promise of spiritual and consented to the covenant. But away with this insane and dangerous opinion - that the Lord promised the Jews, or that they sought for themselves, nothing but a full belly, delights of the flesh, nourishing wealth, outward power, fruitfulness of offspring, and whatever the natural man prizes! Christ the Lord promises to his followers today no other "Kingdom of Heaven," than that in which they may "sit at table with Abraham, Isaac, and Jacob" (Matt.8:11). Peter declared that the Jews of his day were heirs of the grace of the gospel because they were "the sons of the prophets, included in the covenant which the Lord of old made with his people" (Acts 3:25). That this might not be attested in words only, the Lord also approved it by deed. At the moment of his resurrection, he deemed many of the saints worthy of sharing in his resurrection and let them be seen in the city of Jerusalem (Matt.27:52-53). In this he has given a sure pledge that whatever he did or suffered in acquiring eternal

Fudge on the Old Testament

salvation pertains to the believers of the Old Testament as much as to ourselves. Truly, as Peter testifies, they were endowed with the same Spirit of faith whereby we are reborn into life (Acts 15:8). We hear that that Spirit who is like a spark of immortality in us, and for this reason is called in another place the "guarantee of our inheritance" (Eph.1:14), dwelt in like manner in them. How, then, dare we deprive them of the inheritance of life? All the more amazing that the Sadducees of old fell into such stupidity as to deny both the resurrection (Matt. 22:23; Acts 23:8) and the existence of souls, after the Scripture had sealed both doctrines with clear testimonies! Nor would the obtuseness of the whole Jewish nation today in awaiting the Messiah's earthly kingdom be less monstrous, had the Scriptures not foretold long before that they would receive this punishment for having rejected the gospel. For it so pleased God in righteous judgment to strike blind the minds of those who by refusing the offered light of heaven voluntarily brought darkness upon themselves. Therefore, they read Moses and continually ponder his writings, but they are hampered by a veil from seeing the light shining in his face (II Cor.3:13-15). Thus, Moses' face will remain covered and hidden from them until it be turned to Christ, from whom they now strive to separate and withdraw it as much as they can.

I must point out how a little slip in careful thinking causes Fudge to err even when partly correct and

Fudge on the Old Testament

instructive. His conclusion slips by slipping in that one unjustified word "exclusive." "There simply is no basis for making Sheol an <u>exclusive</u> place of punishment for the wicked." By making this incorrect observation, Fudge imagines that he has destroyed an argument for "Sheol" as <u>ever</u> a reference to hell. But no one is claiming that the <u>exclusive</u> meaning of hell may be assigned to Sheol. The KJV avoids that error translating "grave" where the context does not intimate any judgment, whether condemnation or vindication. By that one little carelessness, Fudge misses a large body of Old Testament teaching about Sheol meaning far more than mere "gravedom."

Unfortunately, carelessness of thinking not infrequently appears in this generally learned volume. In fact, the futility of its argument, in spite of much useful research, primarily rests here. If slips in careful deducing can occur in a conscientious and serious scholar, what havoc will it produce among careless readers, much less involved with precise analysis of meaning? And all of this having to do with eternal destiny!

In the following paragraphs on "Sheol's inhabitants," Fudge gives a fine summary of contemporary scholarship on that subject. Again he deduces from his research (as some of those researched also do) *non sequiturs* because they accord with his conditional immortality thinking. For example, he says, "Sheol is

Fudge on the Old Testament

the common fate of all mortals" (85) which is true (of Sheol as the point of death or "gravedom"). "It is not a place of punishment," which is false. Fudge's own citations show that Job calls it a "land of gloom and deep shadow," David "the place of darkness." <u>The Jewish Encyclopedia</u>, "Sheol is a horrible, dreary, dark, disorderly land."(83) Such descriptions do not preclude suffering and punishment. If anything, they imply it. If anything, they imply eternal suffering because no termination is mentioned and all agree that misery, according to the Old and New Testaments alike, never occurs apart from sin. Once again the KJV's translation of Sheol meaning "hell" in certain contexts is justified. Nothing that Fudge or others say rules that out, and over-all biblical theology favors it.

Fudge is more comfortable finding Sheol associated with heaven. "Righteous men and women repeatedly express confidence that God will restore them from Sheol to enjoy life in His fellowship once more (1 Sam.2:6; Ps. 16:9-11; 68:20)." As we said above, Sheol often is associated with hell for the wicked and heaven for the righteous. Any suffering of death would be temporary for those who are "confident that God will restore them...." For those who go down to Sheol in judgment, no such restoration makes the grave a path to glory. Rightly, Fudge observes that the hope of the righteous "is stated explicitly a few times

Fudge on the Old Testament

but it pervades the entire Old Testament."(85) On the other hand, "the wicked have no reason to expect to leave Sheol in <u>most</u> of the Old Testament." Well said, except for the word I underlined, "most." Fudge will vainly try to show us in the next chapter where, in the Old Testament, the wicked have reason to expect to leave the condemnation associated with their Sheol. In a text which is not discussed, we have a reflected ray of light on what Sheol must have meant to the saints in the Old Testament. *"Precious in the sight of the Lord is the death of His saints."* (Ps.116:15) If their death was precious in the sight of the Lord, how precious must it have been to the "saints" of the Old Testament? This is the Old Testament version of Phil.1:21: *"For to me to live is Christ and to die is gain."* David anticipates <u>heaven</u> in Ps.23:6, *"I will dwell in the house of the Lord forever,"* as Paul anticipates <u>Sheol</u> in 2 Tim.4:6-8:

> 6. For I am ready to be offered, and the time of my departure is at hand.
> 7. I have fought a good fight, I have finished my course, I have kept the faith:
> 8. Henceforth there is laid up for me a crown of righteousness, which the Lord, the righteous judge, shall give me at that day: and not to me only, but unto all them also that love his appearing.

Fudge on the Old Testament

Before Fudge studies "The end of the wicked in the Old Testament," he already draws the wrong conclusion in a series of preliminary sentences:

> We are still in the dark concerning life and immortality until Jesus brings them to light in the gospel (2 Tim.1:10). It is no less true that God's wrath also is hidden until it is revealed in the gospel (Rom.1:15-18). Some one has said that the Old Testament is the New Testament <u>concealed</u>, while the new is the Old <u>revealed</u>"(87).

As I observed before, the difference is not between total darkness and total light, but dim candle and brilliant bulb. Just so, Romans 1:15-18 does not say that no wrath is revealed in the Old Testament. Augustine, the "someone" alluded to is better translated "latent" in the Old Testament and "patent" in the New, for he, too, stressed a great difference of degree but not total difference of kind between the two testaments (<u>City of God,</u> 16.26).

Fudge cites the Seventh-Day Adventist LeRoy Froom, who gives seventy English expressions for the Old Testament describing the wicked's termination, which are not endless punishment. Fudge comments on the "cumulative impact" of these citations. The "cumulative impact" of a thousand texts which do <u>not</u> allude to endless punishment is zero to one which

Fudge on the Old Testament

does. To have any effect, texts must <u>preclude</u> eternal punishment, not merely not <u>include</u> it.

Fudge then proceeds to examine Old Testament passages under three headings. The first group contains "moral principles of divine judgment" (90). The Poetic Books, specifically numerous Psalms, teach that the wicked go down to death and Sheol and do not refer to the other world (90). But, as observed above, often when the wicked go down to death and Sheol, it is intimated to be the judgment of an angry God.

Wrath is implied, though not stated, in many passages. As the Westminster Confession teaches, the "whole counsel of God is either expressly set down in Scripture, or by good and necessary consequence may be deduced from Scripture" (I,6). We may "deduce" that a God who takes vengeance (Rom.12:19), will by no means clear the guilty (Num.14:18), and cannot be escaped though we make our bed in hell (Ps.139:8), will after Sheol (death) pay the wages of sin. Even if the Poetic Books did "not specifically threaten a resurrection of the wicked, or any ultimate punishment beyond temporal death itself," they allow for ultimate punishment and do not preclude a bodily resurrection.

Psalm 11:1-7 at the end of the passage asserts that *"On the wicked He will rain fiery coals and burning sulfur...."* Jude tells us that in the fire and brimstone on Sodom and Gomorrah (which carried those people

Fudge on the Old Testament

down to Sheol), they were "undergoing a <u>punishment</u> of <u>eternal</u> fire" (vs.7).

If Fudge says that is New Testament teaching, I grant it. But the infallible New Testament teaches us the meaning of the infallible Old Testament. In case we missed it when we read Genesis, Jude tells us the meaning of what we read. The Apostles missed the Old Testament teaching about the sacrifice of the Messiah, and the Lord took them over the Old Testament, showing them what they had missed (Luke 24:13ff).

Would anyone suggest that Lot did not realize that there was more in the disaster of Sodom and Gomorrah than met the eye? Abraham had pled that the city be spared if there were ten righteous in it (Gen.18:32). Sodom and Gomorrah were destroyed because there were not even ten righteous in the wicked cities and Lot himself had four in his family. So we know that all the inhabitants of Sodom and Gomorrah went down not only to temporal fire and brimstone but to "eternal fire." Later, Sodom and Gomorrah is discussed more fully in <u>The Fire that Consumes</u> upon which I will comment more fully.

Fudge feels explicit support for his heresy in Psalm 24:16 which he cites as saying that in the world to come "the wicked will be <u>no more,</u> (vs.16) this is God's word on the matter, and He will bring it to pass"

Fudge on the Old Testament

(92). Oddly enough the NASV, RSV, KJV, and NIV do not have this Psalm saying that the wicked will be <u>no more</u>, and the Hebrew does not require it. Moreover, even if the expression "no more" is assumed, it would apply to this world and not necessarily to the next. As a matter of fact, there are intimations in the Psalm that the wicked will continue because their memory is only cut off from the <u>earth</u> (22:16) and they are not to cease at death or Sheol, for God "shall slay the wicked" (vs.21), and only those who take refuge in the Lord will be <u>uncondemned</u> (vs.22, emphasis mine).

Other Psalms are studied, with an equal lack of cogency for the matter in question, whereupon our author comes to a summary. Again he makes a point of the fact that the Psalms frequently say that the wicked will "disappear," "not be found," their "name not found in the register of the living," all referring to this world. These passages, Fudge continues, "say nothing of conscious, unending torment...." All Fudge proves is that much of the poetic literature does not "make patent" what is at least latent. There is, we all admit, a real difference between latent and patent; but, not a difference of kind. There is no dispute on this. Where Fudge is cogent in his reasoning is when he proves what is not in dispute.

Next, Fudge considers passages describing specific divine judgments in space-time history. (p.96ff)

Fudge on the Old Testament

The flood is discussed with no significant point being made in the debate.

Then our author focuses on Sodom and Gomorrah. Here Fudge compounds his felony. He sees in the cities' destruction being "perpetual" only once-for-all, supporting it by the fallacious earlier handling of Christ's "everlasting punishment." Christ's everlasting punishment was interpreted as everlasting in the sense that it never lasted a moment after it occurred (everlasting effect of punishment, not everlasting punishment)! And so with the destruction of Sodom and Gomorrah, including Jude's inspired interpretation of it as "eternal fire" (v.7). Jude's "eternal fire," also, is a fire that only burned once and then was eternally finished, the exact opposite of the language used. Jude meant, when he used the expression "eternal fire," that the fire that was temporary for the two earthly cities became "eternal" for its inhabitants. An "eternal fire" does not go out. If it goes out, as Fudge's does, it is not an eternal fire, only eternal ashes.

I was amused to read that we have already seen how the New Testament applies the adjective "eternal to the results of a process, and that fits all the evidence here as well." I agree that it fits "as well" one place as another because it does not fit either (as shown above, with more to follow). We are going to see Fudge try to prove that Jesus' "everlasting punishment" (Matt.

Fudge on the Old Testament

25:46) means only that the punishment of Gehenna was once for all and then the result was "everlasting punishment," meaning the ashes of the consumed were everlasting. But here we have the plain expression "eternal fire" and Fudge simply renders it "temporal fire." This is worse than making the Word of God of "none effect." It makes it of opposite effect.

The Messianic Psalm 1:3-6 is seen as representing the wicked whose "path will finally perish. The picture is one of exclusion, expulsion, disintegration and desolation at that the Psalm stops." (107) The Psalm may stop, but what it teaches keeps on going. *"God knows the way of the righteous,"* but, by contrast, *"the way of the wicked perishes."* Dr. Fudge himself does not believe that the way of the wicked perishes when he dies. He thinks the wicked will not perish until their sins are adequately punished. So do the orthodox. The only difference is that Fudge thinks adequate punishment for a life of sin against an infinite God is some finite time period while the orthodox see guilt against an infinite being itself infinite. Punishment must, therefore, go on forever.

Though the orthodox generally (Augustine, Calvin, Edwards) hold firm on this thinking, some, such as Strong, give up this particular argument while holding to the doctrine. Thus Strong cites Shedd as saying "killing a dog is as bad as killing a man, if merely the

Fudge on the Old Testament

subject who kills and not the object killed is considered" (Dogmatic Theology 2, 740). For Shedd it makes an infinite difference when the killing is aimed at God and not a dog or even a man. Then Strong cites the Simon (Reconciliation) rejoinder that this view "logically requires us to say that trust or reverence or love towards God are infinite, because God is infinite." This makes Strong retreat to what he considers a more impregnable fortress:

> We therefore regard it as more correct to say, that sin as a finite act demands finite punishment, but as endlessly persisted in demands an endless, and in that sense an infinite, punishment.
> (Systematic Theology, 1051)

But Simon could be answered simply by saying that "trust, or reverence, or love" do in heaven receive an endless reward. Why would sin not receive an endless punishment?

Does the Psalm really "stop" with the "exclusion, expulsion, disintegration and desolation" of the "wicked?" If it does, it is stopping with death. That is the perishing which Fudge thinks is the end of the wicked - termination of their being. The "exclusion, expulsion, disintegration and desolation" is their death, according to Fudge. "The way of the wicked will

Fudge on the Old Testament

perish" means nothing more than termination of being.

This would suit the wicked perfectly. They have no desire to be with the righteous even in this world. They do their best to destroy them (Ps.7:1; 31:15; Matt.5:11; 10:23; Luke 21:12; Rom.12:14). They love the "path of sinners" and "the seat of scoffers" is their delight. They may like to go on in their chosen way a little longer but, at least, they have nothing to fear. Ceasing to exist may deprive them of some pleasure but it also will end the gout. Meanwhile, they may knock off a few more "saints."

The "righteous," who are always crying *"How long, O Lord, how long?"* (Ps.13:1, 35:17; 94:3; Rev.6:9,10), are being told by Fudge's Psalm 1, "until the wicked die." No deliverance ever. Only the disappearance of the unrighteous. No condemnation for the wicked. No vindication for the righteous. "After the ungodly flourish a little longer as a green bay tree I'll snuff them," God is supposed to be saying. The wages of their sin will be eternal oblivion. That's my divine "vengeance."

The ultimate wrong in this travesty on Psalm 1 is that "perishing" would be the same end for the righteous. The Psalm says that the Lord "knows" their way, but that does not delete Fudge's Sheol. Knowing their way, as Fudge interprets it, literally says nothing about their future.

Fudge on the Old Testament

As far as anything the Psalm **literally** expresses there is the same future for the sheep and the goats. Instead of one group going to heaven and the other to hell, both perish, PERIOD. On Fudge's thin exegesis the righteous and wicked would end the same way: "exclusion, expulsion, disintegration and desolation." The dead do not rise, according to Fudge's Psalm 1, and, according to 1 Corinthians 15:19, that would make the godly "of all men most to be pitied."

Of course, Fudge does believe in a future resurrection of the righteous, based on other texts. But so far as Psalm 1 is concerned, and the Old Testament generally, there is no such consolation for the righteous. The resurrection will come as a pleasant surprise for Old Testament saints, though one individual, Job, did express a pious hope that something like that would happen someday (19:25).

Isaiah 33:10-14 is another passage where Fudge takes the everlastingness out of the "everlasting." *"Who among us can live with everlasting burning?"* (vs.14) Fudge: "The 'everlasting burning' of Isaiah 33:14 parallels the 'consuming fire' of verse 11, and both refer best to God in His holiness." (109) God in His holiness, justice and wrath indeed becomes a consuming fire of everlasting burning. The burning is clearly a judgment of God revealing His character. Earlier, Fudge had remarked: "The 'fire' of this

Fudge on the Old Testament

passage does not preserve - it consumes! That is why no wicked person can 'dwell' with it."

Here again we have the exact opposite of the manifest meaning. Instead of the fire consum*ing* it has consum*ed* and now is out; a non-burning "everlasting burning." Isaiah's wicked cannot "dwell" with it because it is so overwhelming. For Fudge, they cannot dwell with it because there is nothing to dwell with - the fires are out and the victims have been annihilated.

Fudge's notion of temporary post-death punishment, however, inconsistently assumes that the wicked *can* "dwell" with the "everlasting burning" for awhile. Fudge's consuming fire does *not* really, in any sense, consume or burn them up or it would be nothing but a momentary unfelt experience.

If one were told that when the dentist hits a nerve it will destroy it instantly, and there will be no feeling in that nerve then or ever again, there would be no fear of the needle hitting the nerve. The Bible says of the wicked that there is no fear of God before their eyes (Ps.36:1). Fudge gives the wicked a biblical basis for their attitude! But just as the wicked are about to sigh with complete relief, Fudge introduces a temporary punishment and spoils their fun a little. When assured there is no eternal punishment, they are quickly restored to living it up again.

If God were Fudge's kind of consuming fire, no

Fudge on the Old Testament

wicked person need ever fear it or Him. The sinner might not wish to die, but he would have no terror of God's way of execution. Painless dentistry. Painless pain. Everlasting burning that destroys before it burns. Everlasting punishment without any punishment ever. "The 'everlasting burning' of this passage does not torment perpetually." (109) Indeed, it does not torment at all. It is over before the wink of an eye. The eye and all is gone before it can wink.

It is a relatively minor matter, but let me point out that if Fudge's interpretation were consistent, it would imply annihilation and not Fudge's conditionalism. God's judgment, "the fire that consumes," must be instantaneous or eternal and its effect cannot be temporary. God's wrath is infinite; but now held in check by His "forbearance" until it is meted out (Rom.2:4). Once this vengeance is meted out it would destroy completely. "If thou, Lord shouldest...mark iniquities, O Lord, who shall stand?" (Ps.130:3)

Fudge's own "everlasting burning," like his "everlasting punishment," is a contradiction in terms - Paradox Eschatology. Remember that his ever-burning fire is the divine wrath that "consumes" sinners.

First, if it does literally consume or destroy the impenitent, surely that would have to be instantaneous. It would not only instantly destroy the wicked but also instantly destroy Fudge's conditionalism, which

Fudge on the Old Testament

has sinners being unconsumed for some undefined period of time. Nebuchadnezzar had his fiery furnace heated "seven times more than it was usually heated" (Dan.3:19), so as to consume Shadrach, Meschach and Abednego more fiercely and quickly. In comparison with God as consuming fire, Nebuchadnezzar's furnace would not equal the striking of a match.

Second, since this ever-burning fire is for the sole purpose of consuming sinners which it would accomplish instantly, it would go out just as instantly. It would be a never-burning fire. The wicked may shrink from death not because of death but because of the possible pain connected with it or after it. That would not be a possibility with Fudge's "consuming fire." Many would flee to it, not from it. It is peace forever; not wrath ever. The suicide's desire.

Since God will not clear the guilty, apart from repentance and faith in Christ, the impenitent must be adequately punished. But that spells eternal punishment and not temporal punishment such as conditionalism anticipates. Sin against an infinite being has to be realized fully by a temporal being so punishment must go on eternally without ever being fully satisfied. There is no way it can ever end. It is all or nothing. Orthodox eternal punishment or no punishment at all.

We know that God will not clear the guilty. He will

Fudge on the Old Testament

not acquit them by disregarding their guilt or withhold punishment by annihilating them. Since God will not clear the guilty, they must be punished eternally. Anything less than that would not be adequate. God is incapable of doing anything inadequate, improper, unjust, insufficient. It is sin that "misses the mark" (1 Tim.6:20), and God is no sinner.

One of the most explicit of Old Testament statements about hell is found in Isaiah 66:23-24:

> 23. And it shall come to pass, that from one new moon to another, and from one sabbath to another, shall all flesh come to worship before me,' saith the Lord.
> 24. And they shall go forth, and look upon the carcasses of the men that have transgressed against me: for their worm shall not die, neither shall their fire be quenched; and they shall be an abhorring unto all flesh.'

Dr. Fudge recognizes that:

> Jesus quotes these words in one of His own famous statements about final punishment (Mark 9:48), and they have formed the bases for much Christian teaching on hell ever since. (111)

He therefore considers the passage carefully. For one thing, the righteous behold:

Fudge on the Old Testament

> the dead bodies of the wicked. They look at corpses...not living people. They view their destruction, not their misery....Because this fire is 'not quenched' or extinguished, it completely consumes what is put in it. Because of worms this is a 'loathsome' scene. The righteous view it with disgust but not pity. The <u>final</u> picture is one of shame, not pain.

Fudge continues:

> Traditional writers, as a matter of course, interpret this passage in light of their conception of final punishment rather than forming an understanding on the basis of the passage. (112)

The analysis of this passage seems common sensical and according to a common experience of people being gratified to see the corpses of enemies marking their own success in battle. The casual reader would wonder where the "traditionalists" ever did get the idea of an ever-burning hell from a valley of corpses, says Fudge.

But when one looks at the scene Isaiah presents, the whole point is that these are no ordinary "carcasses," but "carcasses" that do not die. Their worm does <u>not</u> die and their fire is <u>not</u> quenched. When corpses are consumed naturally by worms, the worms then die for want of food; or, when fire burns corpses,

Fudge on the Old Testament

the fire goes out because the corpses are consumed. But these worms do not die and this fire keeps burning.

The worms do not die and the fire is not quenched because these dead people are not dead! They are the burning "dead" in torment. Traditionalists do not "interpret this passage in light of their conceptions," but this passage, and Christ's interpretation of it produce their conceptions. One does not have to be a traditionalist to see that "carcasses" which do not die are ever-living "carcasses."

One can believe Isaiah and Jesus Christ or not but he cannot fail to get the message. Even the commentator in the usually liberally-oriented Speaker's Bible reluctantly grants that the sombre interpretation of Jesus' words (Mark 9:44), is undoubtedly valid:

> the Exegesis says that the substance goes back to Jesus undoubtedly. At least this saying calls for a stress on the eternal validity of the distinction between good and evil, a distinction which is too often blurred when the idea of the eternal consequences of evil-doing drops out of man's thinking. (793)

Fudge's own interpretation shows its inconsistency more clearly here than in some other places. Note: "Because this fire is not 'quenched' or extinguished, it completely consumes what is put in it...."

Fudge on the Old Testament

Precisely because the fire is not "quenched," it does not "completely consume" what is put in it. If it did "completely consume" everything, the fire would go out, would be quenched. The very point of the passage is that it does not go out. Nor does the worm die. The fire Fudge is thinking of does go out because there is nothing left to burn. His worm does die. Fudge completely reverses Isaiah's (and Christ's) point.

Also verse 23 is forgotten:

> And it shall come to pass, from one new moon to another, and from one sabbath to another, shall all flesh come to worship before me, says the Lord.

Undoubtedly, this refers to the admittedly eternal life of the saints who contemplate the eternal death of the transgressors. And, as Fudge correctly observes, "with disgust and not pity;" plus what Fudge cannot see: glorifying the power, wrath, justice, and holiness of God.

I will not take the time to critique the handling of other Old Testament texts or the inter-testamental literature. Our author gives more of the same type of exposition. "God will judge," Fudge concludes, "the wicked by destroying them not eternally but instantly and utterly" (and thus immorally, I must add). Fudge leaves no room for his own notion of a temporal punishment following death because, "destroying

Fudge on the Old Testament

them not eternally but <u>instantly</u> and utterly" destroys even the temporary punishment of his conditionalistic view. I have tried to show above that this is not an interpretation of the Old Testament, but the avoiding of one.

The very important point that Fudge makes about the inter-testamental literature is:

> We must deny categorically the common assumption that Jesus' hearers all held to everlasting torment. We must not assume that Jesus endorsed such a view simply because He nowhere explicitly denied it. (154)

We will let this matter go (though I may mention Morey's thorough refutation of Fudge, p.119ff), not because it is not interesting and important, but because it is not necessary for the refutation of Fudge's interpretation of the New Testament data, to which we now come.

CHAPTER 6
JESUS' TEACHING ABOUT HELL

In Matthew 5:22, Jesus says that *"anyone who says, 'you fool!' will be in danger of the fire of hell."* Says Fudge, "This is the Savior's first specific reference to Gehenna, by now a technical term in Jewish sources for the fiery pit in which the godless will meet their final doom." (159)

Jesus describes this valley outside Jerusalem where the constant debris of the metropolis kept the worms ever living and the fires never dying. Fudge grants that this "Gehenna would convey a sense of total horror and disgust. Beyond that, however, one must speak with extreme caution." (161)

But why the "extreme caution" when it is indubitable that, according to Jesus, sinful persons are going to be cast into a place of everlasting burning? If the imagery does not say that, what does it say? How can it not say the one thing it represents - perpetual burning? If one is to be cautious about accepting the obvious and indubitable, when may he be confident? Fudge describes this Gehenna as loathsome and abhorrent, we must remember, but Fudge's Gehenna is the place where nothing but the <u>effect</u> of the punishment remains, not the punishing itself. After a relatively short while without any "fuel" Gehenna

Jesus' Teaching About Hell

continues eternally to burn and smoke while its worms live without food for ever and ever. That is, according to Edward William Fudge it does. According to Orthodoxy, Jesus gives a reason why the worms do not die and the fire does not go out.

In the handling of Matthew 5:25, 26:

> Settle matters quickly with your adversary who is taking you to court. Do it while you are still with him on the way, or he may hand you over to the judge, and the judge may hand you over to the officer, and you may be thrown into prison. I tell you the truth, you will not get out until you have paid the last penny.

We have Fudge the non-interpreting interpreter again. He notes that there are diverse interpretations of the man who must remain in prison until he has paid the "last penny." But there is no question that the Judge is God and the prisoner is the sinner. How does the sinner ever pay God the last penny he owes Him? This is a punishment scene and, since it deals with an impenitent sinner in the world where conversion and salvation no longer occur, what will he do but everlastingly resent the divine wrath, as he does in this world, thus heaping up wrath rather than paying it off?

I note fellow conditionalist Guillebaud's interpretation which Fudge approves:

Jesus' Teaching About Hell

> A prisoner who never comes out of prison does not live there eternally. The slave who was delivered to the tormentors till he should pay two million pounds would not escape from them by payment, but he would assuredly die in the end: why should not the same result be at least a possibility in the application. (165)

Why not? Because we are not here dealing with an earthly Judge, an earthly prison, or a prisoner on this earth.

I would let Fudge's inadequate handling of Matthew 7:13, 14 go except that he actually tries to enlist it in support of his conditionalist view. The broad road that leads to destruction is explained this way: ". . . Jesus offers us a choice: persecution now or destruction hereafter. To be thrown into Gehenna (Matt. 5: 29,30) is the 'destruction' of this text. Or, to say it in the other direction, those thrown into hell will be destroyed."(167) Once again the place of eternal burning, eternal destruction and eternal punishment means nearly instant extinction. Destruction and eternal destruction; fire and eternal fire; punishment and eternal punishment, are not synonyms. Note, too, that according to this interpretation, Christians suffer persecution in this world while Fudge's wicked receive none in this evil world or in the next.

I find it significant that Dr. Fudge very infrequent-

Jesus' Teaching About Hell

ly mentions his own view of temporal punishment in the next world. The almost exclusive concentration is on the effect of the destruction not on the duration of the punishment even in his own view of limited punishment. At times, as we have seen, his language even excludes <u>any</u> future punishment. He may sense that if he keeps mentioning that those thrown into <u>his</u> Gehenna will not be destroyed instantly it will be apparent that his "once-for-allness" destruction versus "eternal" destruction does not stand up. It is supposed to be a contrast between a relatively brief versus endless punishment; not the eternal punishment of the orthodox versus the no punishment of the consistent heretics, the annihilationists.

Let me repeat that unlike the annihilationists' view which Fudge recognizes to be erroneous, his own view favors a time of punishment after death. That means that for Fudge, Gehenna has some meaning. It is a part-time Gehenna for sinners. It is not, as represented in Scripture, a full-time, eternal Gehenna.

This is an untenable interpretation, though. Fudge does make Gehenna a Gehenna if only for a while. But for a while it is a place of <u>punishing</u>, not merely a place of <u>punishment</u>, the <u>result</u> of punishing. His interpretation makes Gehenna a place of temporal punishing but he admits that the Gehenna of Jesus Christ is eternal. Thus he contradicts the eternality of Christ's

Jesus' Teaching About Hell

Gehenna and is inconsistent with his own view of a temporary punishing.

In summary:

1. Fudge interprets the Lord's Gehenna as eternal.
2. However, this eternal Gehenna Fudge considers eternal only as the <u>effect</u> of punishing.
3. But the effect of the temporal punishing is no further punishing ever in Gehenna. Gehenna's fire is quenched and its worms die.
4. Fudge's temporal Gehenna is unlike the Christ's eternal Gehenna.
5. Thus Fudge contradicts his Lord Jesus Christ.

Fudge may critique my analysis of his teaching this way. He may say that he is not differing with Christ in His interpretation of Gehenna. He is simply stating something implicit in the Lord's teaching. Fudge thinks that Gehenna has two periods. The first period is the period of punish<u>ing</u>. The second period is the period of punish<u>ment</u>. The first period of Gehenna is temporal. The second period is everlasting. Christ's eternal Gehenna is referring only to

Jesus' Teaching About Hell

Gehenna's second, eternal period of punish<u>ment</u>, whereas the orthodox Gehenna mentions the first period of punish<u>ing</u>, which period Christ does mention. So I, Fudge, do not - perish the thought - contradict my Lord but simply add an aspect of Gehenna which is implicit in Christ's teaching but not here expressed.

I feel certain that is Fudge's intention and I honor him for his intention. But it is not sound thinking and I defend my analysis which this statement does not refute. It does not refute it because the only Gehenna of which the Lord speaks is an eternal Gehenna. That carries no implication that there is ever a merely temporal or temporal phase of Gehenna. A temporal Gehenna is the opposite of an eternal Gehenna not a phase of it. Temporal and eternal are mutually exclusive terms; that which is temporal is not eternal; that which is eternal is not temporal. Remember also that in Christ's Gehenna the worm does not die and the fire is not quenched. In Fudge's Gehenna the worm has to die and the fire has to go out which also shows that it is not the Gehenna of Jesus Christ.

The choice here is not between the conditionalist and the orthodox, but again between the annihilationist and the orthodox. The conditionalist is in no-sinner's land. Either there is a Gehenna as Jesus teaches or there is not as the annihilationist teaches.

Jesus' Teaching About Hell

These are meaningful opposites, true choices, mutually exclusive options. If Christ is right, the annihilationist is wrong. If the annihilationist is right, the Lord Jesus Christ is wrong. And, of course, if the Lord Jesus Christ is wrong He is not the Lord Jesus Christ.

Matthew 7:19: *"Every tree that does not bear good fruit is cut down and thrown into the fire."* In a sermon in which Gehenna (the fire which is always burning), is twice mentioned by name, can the hearers think that this bad tree "thrown into the fire" is thrown into any fire but the eternal fire of Gehenna?

We know that Fudge would see in the house built on the sand, which fell when the storms came (Matt.7:27), a house falling suddenly and once for all (especially since the NIV has the house falling "immediately"- "the moment the torrent struck"). Is comment necessary, especially inasmuch as Fudge's Gehenna implies some punishing?

If so, let me simply say that Christ's teaching throughout the Sermon on the Mount is that following Him in the narrow way leads to eternal life. Taking the broad way leads to Gehenna. If one's house is built on His words it will survive the Day of Judgment. If not, it will fall into Gehenna, "immediately"- "the moment the torrent ("judgment") struck." There can be no question about that. The question again is what Jesus

Jesus' Teaching About Hell

meant by "Gehenna." We have seen the difference between the orthodox and conditionalist interpretations. I think that the orthodox and conditionalist will agree: whoever is right about Gehenna, his interpretation here is also correct and vice versa.

"Weeping and gnashing of teeth." Fudge examines the seven gospel references to this experience which traditionalism sees as a reference to the everlasting agony of the damned. (171) Our author sees no such thing. Rather, those who weep and gnash teeth do so because they are separated from the blessed and banished from their company. Two passages have them thrown into the "fiery furnace." Fudge finds this not the necessary cause of the weeping and gnashing because it is <u>not</u> mentioned in these other cases. Then he concludes that the weeping comes from the realization that God has thrown them out as worthless "and they anticipate the execution of His sentence." (172)

I ask what that sentence could be but the fiery furnace? The gnashing of teeth indicates the misery of the wicked and their wrath against God and His redeemed:

> The common assumption that 'weeping and gnashing of teeth' describes the everlasting agony of souls in conscious torment is the interpretation of a later age, and it lacks any clear biblical support. (172)

Jesus' Teaching About Hell

As Fudge himself interprets this experience it is the "agony of souls in conscious torment." His only difference with what he calls the "interpretation of a later age" is that the "later age" includes the word everlasting. Fudge himself finds no indication here that it is <u>not</u> everlasting. It is merely his mistaken assumption that the coming punishment, the mere anticipation of which causes the weeping and gnashing, puts an everlasting end to their weeping and gnashing.

Another weakness in Fudge's thinking is also present here. He <u>tends</u> to associate pain exclusively with a physical pain. The real picture of the passages is that the weeping and gnashing wicked are thrown away as worthless <u>except</u> in their burning in the eternal furnace, Gehenna, in which they will weep and gnash their teeth in everlasting torment. On Fudge's interpretation they would not weep and gnash in falling into the furnace for that would be the instantaneous <u>end</u> of the misery that causes the weeping and gnashing.

In fact, if they believed what Fudge believes, that would end their weeping and gnashing <u>now</u>. People do, in this world, dread and/or fulminate against traditional hell, Fudge himself being one example. Conditionalists need not do this, because their "everlasting punishment" is the everlasting end of all punishment

Jesus' Teaching About Hell

and suffering. This "hell" puts an end to orthodox hell and all the weeping and gnashing that goes with even the anticipation of it. Fudge's hell ends all weeping and gnashing of teeth whereas Jesus' hell causes weeping and gnashing of teeth eternally.

Matthew 10:28 - *"Do not be afraid of those who kill the body but cannot kill the soul. Rather, be afraid of the one who can destroy both body and soul in hell."*

Calvin says that this text makes one's hair stand on end. Fudge, however, stands the text on end. It means for Fudge that "only God should be ultimately feared..." (173) and then his interpretation removes that fear of God.

The passage that made Calvin's hair stand on end (Matt.10:28) is reduced to this by Fudge:

> Our Lord's warning is plain. Man's power to kill stops with the body and the horizons of the Present Age. The death man inflicts is not final, for God will call forth the dead from the earth and give the righteous immortality. God's ability to kill and destroy is without limit. It reaches deeper than the physical and further than the present. God can kill both body and soul, both now and hereafter. (p.177)

Christ is not talking about "immortality" in heaven in this text, but divine judgment in hell for those who fear men. Knowing that "God's ability to kill and destroy

Jesus' Teaching About Hell

is without limit" is no terror when the coward is assured it certainly will be limited for him and all the wicked. Interpreting Luke's parallel text, Fudge says, "God first slays His enemies, then throws their dead bodies into the consuming fire." God thus becomes less of a threat than many human torturers. Incidentally, this statement of Fudge is another indication of his implicit annihilationism. If God slays His enemies before He throws their "dead bodies into the consuming fire," then the living wicked never go to Gehenna at all for even temporary punishment. They are already dead when they are cast into Gehenna. This is Richard John Neuhaus's hell which is always burning, but no one ever goes there.

The text says that one should not fear those who can "kill the body." One would normally be afraid of being reduced to "buckwheat" by the mob. This fear, according to Jesus, should be dispelled by the incomparably greater punishment of God who can "kill body and soul" in "hell." But Fudge's God will end all this torment. Logically, one need not fear God at all. Fudge's text should read: "Fear not Him who terminates all suffering. Only fear those who can kill you in this world. If you can escape them you have nothing to fear in the next world."

Fudge's view also makes the person men can kill the same person God can kill. There is no difference.

Jesus' Teaching About Hell

But Christ says there is a difference and emphasizes it. Men can kill the body; but God can kill body "and soul." What God has distinguished and separated (body and soul), Fudge joins together.

Fudge pleads innocent. He points out that this is the way Matthew states it. But Luke puts it differently. He has Jesus saying that God can throw "you" into hell. In Fudge's thinking, the body and soul are not inseparable. The notion that they are came from Plato, not Scripture. So Fudge is not joining together what he thinks God has joined together, but what Plato joined together.

Now we have Fudge versus Fudge. He does not believe that Scripture errs, but he has the Jesus of Luke versus the Jesus of Matthew, or Matthew and Luke against each other.

If Scripture does not err, then Matthew and Luke and Jesus in Matthew and Luke are consistent with each other. But if so, Luke's reference to "you" being cast into hell is harmonious with Matthew's Jesus (even if Jesus happens to agree with Plato), saying that men can kill the body only and not touch the soul which survives the death of the body. But God can kill "body and soul" which must be what Luke meant when his Jesus said that God can kill "you," body <u>and</u> soul implied.

The second difference between man's and God's

Jesus' Teaching About Hell

killing is that the former is confined to this world while God's extends to endless Gehenna. Here, too, Fudge is wresting Scripture. The gospel accounts are making the killings differ not only in nature (body only versus body and soul), but also in duration. Man's punishment of the body is limited to the time of earthly death. God's punishing is endless according to Christ, but not according to Edward William Fudge.

Fudge launches into a heavy critique of traditionalist teaching (173-178). I believe that much of the problem we have with the historic and contemporary attack on hell is that the biblical scholars involved do not think deeply. In this area, they remain scholars of texts but not thinkers about the meaning of the texts they laboriously research. In a sense, the blind are leading the blind and both are falling into the pit of denying the Pit. To be specific, I will cite Fudge's critique here.

There is this "interesting point" according to Mr. Fudge:

> If a man depends wholly on God for his existence day by day, and if the wicked are banished absolutely from God's presence and are deprived of any divine blessing, the question must arise how much they can continue to exist for any period of time.

This seems to Fudge to be a great difficulty for

Jesus' Teaching About Hell

Orthodoxy and leads him to remark that:

> On this matter traditionalist writers have for the most part been strangely silent. When they have spoken, they have often applied to the wicked descriptions of the resurrected body which Paul reserves for the righteous alone. Such an indiscriminate use of terms characterizes the writings of Athenagoras, Augustine, and Chrysostom, and it has been carried on by traditionalist advocates since. Calvin was aware of this problem, though he never seems to have met it head-on. Luther posed the difficult question himself but refused to give it much thought. It has often been observed that his chief concern was justification, not eschatology. Many modern authors, both Catholic and Protestant, seeing no biblical stepladder down from this tightrope, simply leap into the philosophical net of the immortality of the soul.

This being absolutely no problem at all, which Fudge considers insuperable, I wondered where he and Constable, on whom he relies, got that notion of great difficulty. I will not consider every reference the two authors cite in showing this "great difficulty," but it is no great difficulty to show that there is no great difficulty here. A few citations should suffice.

Fudge on Shedd, for example, is just as bewildering as Constable's thinking. I feel like Alice in Wonderland as I read remark after remark made to prove

Jesus' Teaching About Hell

one point that clearly establishes its opposite. Shedd is quoted in a very clear statement of the kind of resurrection the wicked can and will have in accordance with his orthodox view that leads Fudge to claim virtual admission of his (Fudge's) opinion: "This being the case, does it not follow that the wicked, deprived of any life from God and subjected to the destructive force of Gehenna besides, will eventually lose all vitality and truly die?" (176)

Here are the Shedd citations which are supposed to lead to that conclusion:

> W.G.T. Shedd, a powerful advocate of everlasting conscious torment, made the same point, which he never entirely reconciled with his overall conclusion. In The Doctrine of Endless Punishment Shedd wrote: The bodies of the wicked, on the contrary, are not delivered from the power of Sheol, or the grave, by a blessed and glorious resurrection, but are still kept under its dominion by a "resurrection to shame and everlasting contempt" (Dan. 12:2). Though the wicked are raised from the dead, yet this is no triumph for them over death and the grave. Their resurrection bodies are not 'celestial' and 'glorified,' like those of the redeemed, but are suited to the nature of their evil and malignant souls. (176)

Fudge is thinking that "resurrection bodies" suited to their "evil and malignant souls" must tend to death

Jesus' Teaching About Hell

while Shedd is affirming exactly the opposite - they are "<u>resurrected</u> bodies." Paul also looked for a "resurrection of both the just and the unjust" (Acts 24:15) though he speaks of the unjustified as suffering "the punishment of <u>eternal</u> destruction..." (2 Thess.1:9; emphasis mine). Surely God, in whom the wicked live, move, and have their being in this world (Acts 17:28), can continue to preserve them in the world to come and in their resurrected bodies for the purpose of suffering their deserved punishment. His wrath rests upon them even now. (John 3:36) Why not later? They are only separated communally, not existentially.

According to Fudge:

> May we not think of a glowing ember which, removed from the fireplace, finally loses all its fire? Or can we compare the case to an electric heater, now unplugged from its source of power, which glows for a short period of time but finally and inevitably goes out?

Think of an ember which loses all its fire or an unplugged heater? Of course we cannot because God has given the wicked <u>resurrection</u> bodies so that they <u>cannot</u> die. As I said, they are not separated from God existentially, but only communally. Where, O where, is any problem? Ironically, the problem is Fudge's not Shedd's. How could a damned soul or body exist one

Jesus' Teaching About Hell

moment if God withdrew His power from them as Fudge imagines He does in Fudge's temporary Gehenna? The real horror of hell is not the metaphysical absence of God from hell but His wrathful presence. Scripture asks who can understand the power of His anger, not who can stand under it. (Ps.90:11)

Calvin's Institutes 3. 25. 9: are also cited by Fudge. Let me print the text in question and comment:

> If anyone should object that the resurrection is not fitly conferred by fleeting earthly benefits, my answer is that when they were first cut off from God the fountain of life, they deserved the death of the devil, in which they would be utterly destroyed. Yet by God's wonderful plan, an intermediate state was found, so that apart from life they should live in death. It ought not to seem in any respect more absurd if there is an incidental resurrection to the judgment seat of Christ, whom they now refuse to listen to as their Master and Teacher. For to be consumed by death would be a light punishment if they were not brought before the Judge to be punished for their obstinacy, whose vengeance without end and measure they have provoked against themselves.
>
> But, although we must hold to what we have said and to what that famous confession of Paul before Felix contains - that he awaits a coming resurrection of just and unjust (Acts 25:15) - still Scripture more often sets forth resurrection, along with heavenly glory to the children of God alone.

Jesus' Teaching About Hell

One can see Calvin's answer to the "problem" of the wicked being "blessed" with a resurrection. It is no great "blessing" to be "unwillingly haled before the judgment seat of Christ, whom they now refuse to listen to as their Master and Teacher," by "an incidental resurrection." Calvin compares it to our first parents instead of being destroyed immediately upon sinning being preserved "so that apart from life they should live in death." In other words, resurrection so far from being a problem is the divine solution to how to keep the damned "alive in death" here and in hell. There are blessed resurrection bodies for the saints in heaven and cursed ones for those in hell. Their bodies will, no doubt, be as hideous as their depraved souls and fitted by God for everlasting torment.

Let me next consider Fudge's appeal to the New Catholic Encyclopedia (13:469) :

> **Immortality of the Damned.** The problem of the eternity of hell is also connected with the immortality of the soul. From time to time there has recurred the idea of a conditional immortality. That is, survival after death is conditional on conformity with God's law and wishes. Against the Agnostics, Irenaeus said that the soul is not immortal by nature, but it can become immortal if it lives according to God's law. Arnobius the Elder also held this view; it implies that the damned are not in fact called to immortality. In their eagerness to

Jesus' Teaching About Hell

> point out the salvific significance of immortality, that it is a gratuitous gift and is intended to benefit man, some writers such as Justin and Tatian tended to favor the idea that the souls of the wicked died or were annihilated (thanatopsychism). They did not fully appreciate that the eternal death of which the Apocalypse speaks, i.e. being cut off from God forever, does involve some sort of immortality, although not the immortality intended by God. They did not pay sufficient attention to the fact that man's conduct here on earth decides his lot forever, not only in the sense that he can earn eternal reward but in the sense that he can also earn eternal damnation.

If one reads the above quotation, he will realize the writer is saying that, and explaining how, the Fudge type of teaching has "from time to time" appeared in the church. It was because certain theologians could not see that the souls of the wicked could be made immortal because they wrongly associated immortality exclusively with glorious immortality. Their error was in not seeing that the wicked can "earn eternal damnation," which is "some sort of immortality." The New Catholic Encyclopedia is orthodox on this point.

Jonathan Edwards, who is not here cited by Fudge but is the greatest defender that the orthodox doctrine of hell has ever had, insists that God's presence in hell is what makes hell hell. God is present there to curse

Jesus' Teaching About Hell

the wicked, who exist only by His power, for using that power only to sin. The wicked exist in hell eternally only by the eternal power of God. How the damned do wish that Fudge was right. If only God would withdraw His eternal power so that they could pass into nothing as Fudge so fondly imagines.

In Edwards' words: "'Tis the infinite almighty God that shall become the fire of the furnace." "God will be the hell of one (the wicked) and the heaven of the other (the redeemed)." (Unpublished sermon on II Cor.4:18 (2) p.5 in my Jonathan Edwards on Heaven and Hell, p.57). Eternity for the sinner will be spent "in the immediate presence and sight of God..." (Ibid). It is because God is the fire which burns in hell that words can never convey - much less exaggerate - the terrors of the damned. "Law and gospel both agree that God intends an extraordinary manifestation of His terribleness." (Unpublished sermon on Job 41:9f p.15)

In other words, Constable and Fudge see a problem presumably ignored or unanswered by the orthodox because there is no problem to be answered. Fudge cites sources which prove exactly the opposite of what they are cited to show.

In conclusion to this discussion, Fudge cites a fellow-conditionalist, Gillebaud, who introduces the theme of some degree of torment. "How terrible the process of destruction will be will depend on the

Jesus' Teaching About Hell

degree of each soul's guilt before God." (178) Here again the logic of the conditionalists leads them inevitably to the annihilationism they try to avoid. If God's wrath tends to destroy the sinner in time, why would it not do so immediately? Certainly finite power unaided by the Infinite could never stand against the Infinite for a moment. If, on the other hand, Fudge and others would concede that the person under full divine wrath for a time could be preserved by God for a time, why could God not also preserve the sons of perdition eternally? Once again, it is annihilationism or everlasting preservation with a no-man's land for conditionalists in between.

Fudge does not give up easily. He next cites the conditionalist Henry Constable:

> They (the orthodox) tell us that a change will pass upon the wicked at their resurrection! We ask for proof. They cannot say that there cannot be a resurrection without a change; for, unfortunately for them, there have been resurrections where no change has taken place. All the resurrections before Christ were such. He was the 'first fruits from the dead,' because in the case of others raised before Him no change from mortality took place. They cannot say that there cannot be a resurrection followed by death; for, again, the cases of Jairus' daughter, and the widow's son, and Lazarus, would confront them; for all these, after they were raised, died

again We ask them for proof that the bodies of the wicked will undergo any change at their resurrection. (50)

To this statement, Fudge adds:

> Had Constable lived a hundred years later, he would have found some scholarly support. F.F. Bruce, dean of evangelical scholars, says that it is curious though perhaps accidental 'that in Paul's letters there is no clear reference to the resurrection of the wicked.' (51) Murray Harris, a professor at Trinity Evangelical Divinity School near Chicago, calls it a 'distinctive feature of the Christian view of resurrection' that the righteous dead are transformed as well as revived. He uses the same illustration as Constable in making his point. 'To be revived is not to be resurrected: the raising of Lazarus (Jn.11:1-44) or the widow of Nain's son (Lk.7:11-17) was a restoration to temporary physical life (they came to life ultimately to die once more), not a resurrection to permanent spiritual life.'(52) Harris observes that according to the New Testament there is a reanimation that leads to judgment, not to life but to the 'second death' (Dan.12:2; John 5:29; Rev.20:4-6, 11-25).

Constable asks us for proof that "the bodies of the wicked will undergo <u>any change</u> at their resurrection." Proof? How can there be a resurrection without a change? Does not "resurrection" mean that dead bodies

Jesus' Teaching About Hell

change into living bodies? Granted that there is much more associated with resurrection than that. But is there ever anything less? Constable admits that the "bodies of the wicked" have "their resurrection" and in the same sentence challenges proof that there is <u>any change</u> in the wicked! Non-resurrected bodies cannot become resurrected bodies without "**<u>any change</u>**."

Fudge continues with this incredible remark: "Had Constable lived a hundred years later, he would have found some scholarly support. F.F. Bruce...says...that in Paul's letters there is no clear reference to the resurrection of the wicked."

Bruce's' statement that there is no clear reference to the resurrection of the wicked in <u>Paul's letters</u> is supposed to support Constable's statement that there is <u>no change</u> in the wicked's resurrection. But Bruce is <u>puzzled</u> about no reference in Paul's letters to any resurrection of the wicked and Constable is <u>asserting no change</u> in their resurrection bodies. Bruce is saying in the citation nothing at all about changes or no changes in resurrection bodies of people. In that citation he neither supports nor opposes Constable. Incidentally, in his foreword to this book, Bruce <u>does admit that even Paul teaches</u> the resurrection of the wicked without developing the doctrine in Acts 24:15 (p.viii). So Constable has no argument and Bruce gives him no support.

Jesus' Teaching About Hell

We remind the reader of the nature of this alleged "problem." The conditionalists say that the orthodox do, in spite of the evidence to the contrary, not account for the bodies of the wicked being later in hell, when they themselves admit that the bodies of the wicked are later in hell (for a period). The conditionalists will not speak of the wicked being resurrected for that temporary punishment in hell, but they have no doubt that they will be made alive again - body and soul - for temporary punishment. We noted earlier an inconsistency in Fudge (who had God killing the wicked and then throwing only their bodies into Gehenna), but this should not obscure the general conditionalist doctrine that man is an inseparable body-soul being. Conditionalists do not accept the "Platonic" (biblical) idea of a soul that is separable from the body. (I have refuted that allegation above.) So at death in this world, soul and body die. However, that temporarily non-existent, impenitent sinner is, at the Day of Judgment, going to be raised, tried, found guilty, and punished in Gehenna as long as his accumulated guilt requires. So the conditionalist has no problem with the body-soul totally dead person being "resurrected" or somehow made to live again and in hell, at that. Yet, the orthodox who deny that the soul ever dies, have an immeasurable problem in explaining that God is able to raise mere bodies. And all the while all of us are

Jesus' Teaching About Hell

talking about the Lord God omnipotent!

Fudge then refers to the statement of Professor Harris that Christ's raising the widow of Nain's son and Lazarus from the dead was "not a resurrection to spiritual life." What Harris calls a "distinctive feature of the Christian view of resurrection" is that the "righteous dead are transformed as well as revived." Harris prefers to call these two miracles mentioned above "reanimations" though he does not deny that they were resurrections saying only that they were "not a resurrection to <u>permanent</u> eternal life" (emphasis mine).

Neither Bruce's or Harris's statements deny <u>change</u> in the bodies of the wicked. The fact that at the resurrection the righteous will be perfect in holiness (that change, incidentally, having taken place at death, not at resurrection), does not imply <u>no</u> change in the wicked. They will undergo some kind of non-glorious resurrection with which, according to Conditionalism, their souls are inseparably connected.

What Constable, in particular, is apparently driving at, some of his language notwithstanding, is that Christ is called the *"first fruits of the dead."* (1 Cor.15:20) If He is the first fruits, He must be the first to be resurrected. If Christ were the first to be resurrected, all who were "resurrected" before Him were not resurrected, seems to be the inference.

Jesus' Teaching About Hell

Constable might have noticed that the Bible does not say that Christ's was the first resurrection. He was the "first fruits <u>from the dead</u>." In 1 Corinthians 15:20, Christ is called "the first fruits of those who are asleep." Permanently resurrected persons were not "asleep." Those not yet permanently resurrected were bodily asleep in their graves. They will later be raised as Christ, the first fruits of <u>their</u> resurrection, was. I need not particularly examine them because they do not deal with the one question I consider here, whether the impenitent are punished everlastingly. Consequently, I pass by many texts and pages without comment, the silence meaning neither assent nor dissent.

When Fudge comes again to Matthew 25:41, 46 I will interact because, as he says, these are "perhaps the most famous of all Jesus' words concerning final punishment...." (192) He has already examined this parable (and I with him), and now returns only to look at the "contrast" between "sheep and goats."

Fudge's comment on "eternal fire" is our particular concern. He repeats his insistence that *aionios*, "eternal," means that "its <u>results</u> were to last forever" and I repeat my earlier critiques that it is the punishment, not the result of it, that lasts forever: "everlasting punishment," to be punishment must be punishing.

However, Fudge does not really repeat his argu-

Jesus' Teaching About Hell

ment but his conclusion and then proceeds to the hortatory. The "righteous" are not to take any "ungodly joy at the fate of the wicked."(195) This, of course, is agreed by all. Orthodoxy's argument that *aionios* must have the same meaning for sheep (the righteous) and goats (the unrighteous) does not imply that the redeemed make their blessedness depend on sinners' misery so as to fill them with "ungodly joy at the fate of the wicked." I do not deny that some traditionalists may do this any more than Fudge can deny that some conditionalists may do the same. We both maintain, I trust, that neither traditionalist nor conditionalist is a Christian at all if his joy in Christ Jesus depends on an "ungodly joy at the fate of the wicked."

I do not deny that Orthodoxy sees a godly joy in heaven's contemplating hell not because of the misery of the damned, but because of the justice of God in the inflicting of that misery. Likewise, God does not rejoice in the death of the wicked (Ezek.18:23; 33:11), but in the holiness, righteousness, and justice revealed in their deserved eternal death.

Next comes a learned discussion of *kolasis*, punishment. Fudge concludes that this word, compared with its opposite (the blessing of the righteous), means that the "condemnation" of "shame and everlasting contempt..."(198) is the *kolasis* or punish-

Jesus' Teaching About Hell

ment. Traditionalists, he continues, "sometimes object that irreversible (therefore endless) extinction is actually no 'punishment' at all (ibid) something this traditionalist has contended throughout this book (saying the conditionalist concept is "virtually" rather than "actually" no "punishment").

Fudge proceeds to show what no traditionalist or any other rational person would deny, that most people do shrink somewhat from extinction, even when it is a relief from pain. Then, citing many others, Fudge gets himself into an interesting corner. He sees all whom he cites (Salmond, A.W.Pink, "The Greek Mind," T.H. Huxley, Milton's Belial in Paradise Lost, Witsius, Augustine, Fudge, Constable, and Jonathan Edwards) representing death as a greater punishment than any amount of pain, including eternal. If it were true that termination of life is the ultimate punishment, then the annihilationist (even more than the conditionalist, not to mention the traditionalist), is God's proper benign executioner. Fudge does not feel his discomfiture, so I will leave him in his corner while I try to escape and deliver my fellow traditionalists from that corner where Fudge and those he cites try to put us.

First, let me prove that this apparent corner is no corner at all, and then show that the traditionalists cited - Augustine, Salmon, Pink, Witsius, and Edwards - are misunderstood. The "corner" is that the

Jesus' Teaching About Hell

doctrine of endless hell, God's ultimate punishment approaching the infinite, is actually less than extinction or annihilation. Extinction is no punishment at all because it leaves no one to suffer any punishment. All the relevant illustrations Fudge gives do not prove otherwise. Indeed, they give no evidence whatever. In fact, they are not even dealing with the matter in question. What they concern is the feelings of <u>living</u> people <u>anticipating</u> extinction. <u>They</u> - at least some of them - dread it. They are suffering from the thought of <u>impending</u> extinction, not from <u>extinction</u>. Once extinction comes, all their suffering is over forever. Blessed relief? No, not even that - no feeling; no pleasure; no pain; no nothing. Extinction is the cure of all pain or pleasure, the end of all punishment or vindication.

Salmond's "Greek mind" could very well say - while in this world - that it would prefer "the teeth of Cerferus, or the thickets of the Danaidae, rather than nonentity," but what about the eternal fury of the living God? Does any rational mind ("Greek mind," the barbarian mind, German mind, American mind, or any other mind) imagine it could stand against its Creator? Is Almighty God incapable of making the proud sinner beg for the mountains to fall on him when even human torturers can do as much?

Let me show that the orthodox never taught that

Jesus' Teaching About Hell

annihilation was the equivalent of eternal punishment, though I cannot think of an easier assignment. Since Edwards gives the fullest discussion of the matter in question, let us look and see that he is demolishing what he is supposed to be defending ("Jonathan Edwards, too, concedes this point"). Fudge interprets Edwards' "Concerning the Endless Punishment of Those Who Die Impenitent" as raising "no scriptural objection to eternal extinction" (annihilation). (201) The fact is that Edwards annihilated annihilationism more thoroughly than any Christian theologian in history of whom I am aware. (Compare my A Mini-Theology of Jonathan Edwards, chapter 11 and Jonathan Edwards on Heaven and Hell.)

What, then, does Edwards say in his 15,000 words that Fudge finds raises "no scriptural objections to eternal extinction" (emphasis Fudge's)? I read this essay of Edwards once again and could not find one sentence to justify Fudge's comment. In almost every sentence Edwards, with characteristic profundity, annihilates all forms of annihilation. I will submit merely one paragraph which alone, if understood, would cause Dr. Fudge to throw The Fire that Consumes to the flames:

Jesus' Teaching About Hell

If any should suppose, that the torments of the damned in hell are properly penal, and in execution of penal justice, but yet that they are neither eternal, nor shall end in annihilation but shall be continued till justice is satisfied, and they have truly suffered as much as they deserve, whereby their punishment shall be so long as to be called ever-lasting, but that then they shall be delivered and finally be the subjects of everlasting happiness; and that therefore they shall not be in the mean time in a state of trial, nor will be waited upon in order to repentance, nor will their torments be used as a means to bring them to it; for that the term and measure of their punishment shall be fixed, from which they shall not be delivered on repentance, or any terms or conditions whatsoever, until justice is satisfied: I would observe, in answer to this, that if it be so, the damned, while under their suffering, are either answerable for the wickedness that is acted by them while in that state, or may properly be the subjects of a judicial proceeding for it, or not. If the former be supposed, then it will follow, that they must have another state of suffering and punishment, after the ages of their suffering for the sins of this life, are ended. And it cannot be supposed, that this second period of suffering will be shorter than the first: for the first is only for the sins committed during a short life often represented in Scripture, for its shortness, to be a dream, a tale that is told, a blast of wind, a vapor, a span, a moment, &c. But the time of punishment is always represented as exceeding long, called everlasting; represented as

Jesus' Teaching About Hell

enduring for ever and ever, as having no end, &c. If the sins of a moment must be followed with such punishment, then doubtless, the sins of those endless ages must be followed with another second period of suffering, much longer. For it must be supposed, that the damned continue sinning all the time of their punishment; for none can rationally imagine that God would hold them under such extreme torments, and terrible manifestations and executions of His wrath after they have thoroughly repented, and turned from sin and are become pure and holy, and conformed to God and so have left off sinning. And if they continue in sin during this state of punishment, with assurance that God still has a great benevolence for them, even so as to intend finally to make them everlastingly happy in the enjoyment of His love, then their sin must be attended with great aggravation; as they will have evil and ill desert of sin set before them in the most affecting manner of their dreadful sufferings for it, attended besides with evidence that God is infinitely benevolent towards them, and intends to bestow infinite blessings upon them. But, if this first long period of punishment must be followed with a second as long, or longer, for the same reason the second must by a third, as long, or longer than that; and so the third must be followed by a fourth, and so *in infinitum*; and at this rate there can never be an end of their misery. So this scheme overthrows itself. (Works, Hickman, II, 524)

Fudge summarizes this section saying once again:

Jesus' Teaching About Hell

> the 'eternal punishment' itself is the capital execution, the everlasting loss of the eternal life of joy ...Jude but repeats the Master's thought here when he gives Sodom and Gomorrah as the prototype of those 'who suffer the punishment of eternal fire' (Jude 7), as does Peter in saying that God 'made them an example of what is going to happen to the ungodly' by 'burning them to ashes.'
> (2 Pet. 2:6, 202)

If Fudge had added but three words to that last quotation from Peter to indicate his interpretation, its absurdity would have been even more apparent: "burning them to ashes <u>in eternal fire</u>."

Fudge insists on the "eternal fire" while denying the eternal torment of people in the "eternal fire." If they are burned to ashes (and all of them sometime will be burned to ashes, according to Fudge, all anninihilationists, and all conditionalists), why does the fire go on burning eternally? We traditionalists say that the worm goes on living because there are always "corpses" on which to feed, and the fire is not quenched because there are always corpses to burn. But Fudge's fire is eternal though the worms have died and the flames have been extinguished.

The reader may rightly say to me: You're very repetitious. I plead guilty. But the only way I can account for the deep effect of Fudge's book is its constant reiteration of the same theme of an "eternal

Jesus' Teaching About Hell

punishment" that is not eternal punishment but only the result of eternal punishment. I feel that I have to keep repeating that eternal punishment that is not eternal punishment is not eternal punishment. And since the Word of God incarnate and written insist that the impenitent go into "eternal punishment" and not into eternal results of annihilation, I must keep insisting lest some lost soul some day asks, "Why didn't you warn me?"

Let me add a brief note to Fudge's brief note on John 3:16:

> This favorite verse of so many contrasts 'eternal life' on the one hand with 'perish' on the other. God's love in the gift of His Son guarantees true believers the first; the passage says absolutely nothing to illuminate the second. 'Perish' is a common descriptive verb for the fate of the wicked throughout the Bible. Taken at face value it agrees with all the biblical material we have seen. (208)

The text says "absolutely nothing to illuminate the second" (the perishing) except, I add, that mankind is perishing and continues to perish apart from belief in the Son of God. So the unbelieving go on perishing as long as they go on unbelieving and that is forever. So far as John 3:16 is concerned, the unbelieving perish forever.

Jesus' Teaching About Hell

The rest of the long chapter is worth reading, and further illuminates Fudge's thought with characteristic learning. Since it adds no new argument, however, I feel no need to comment. "Golgotha and Gehenna (Jesus' Death and the Punishment of the Lost)" (215-234) suggests more than it clearly delivers. Christ's death introduces the eschaton or final age and "revealed also what awaits at the end of the world for those who reject Christ now." (221) What that is is not clearly stated.

Toward the end of the chapter, Fudge moves toward our concern as he develops the theme, "Jesus Died the Sinner's Own Death."(226) Finally, Fudge asserts, "Jesus' Death Involved Total Destruction." (228) "Here," says our author, "conditionalists have frequently pounded their pulpits and traditionalists have often crouched down in their pews." His argument is plain and seemingly sound. When Christ paid the penalty of sin for unbelievers, His humanity was destroyed. Ergo, when unbelievers go to hell to suffer God's wrath, they, too, are destroyed.

My first response is that this argument, if sound, would destroy conditionalists as well as traditionalists. Fudge should join us crouching down in his pew. That is, if the punishment of hell is instant extinction, there would be no time for punishment of sins according to degrees of guilt, any more than for an

Jesus' Teaching About Hell

eternal hell.

Second, if the destruction and death of Christ's humanity were the sole price of redemption, His human spirit could not have escaped death nor His body have been resurrected unless God is an "Indian Giver" and devoid of true justice. If "Jesus' Death Involved Total Destruction," Jesus ceased to exist after Calvary. Fudge cannot say, and does not seem to believe, that Jesus was totally and finally destroyed, but was partially and temporally destroyed.

Third, Christ's deity would, according to this view, have played no role in the atonement. If the divine person made the work of Christ's finite nature a thing of infinite value, as Orthodoxy teaches, then any suffering was sufficient, even suffering to the death, but not the extinction, of the body, and Christ in His bodily nature would have been resurrected for His sufferings, not destroyed by them.

Fudge, never intending such a thing, is actually destroying God's atonement just as he has been destroying God's hell. Indeed, because he has been destroying hell he has been destroying heaven, too. "This is the curse of evil deed that of new evil it becomes seed." What happened on Calvary was not that "Jesus' Death Involved Total Destruction." Had it done that, as we said, Jesus would have been but one more of the doomed.

Jesus' Teaching About Hell

What happened throughout Christ's earthly life and especially on the cross was that Jesus was a-dying and finally died in the sense that His human body was temporarily separated from His immortal human spirit. He died as other humans die and in that process He was enduring the wrath of God as other humans do because of the guilt of sin which He incurred vicariously for His people.

The difference is that where other human beings are dead in trespasses and sin and deserve all the sufferings they undergo in this life and eternal damnation afterward, Jesus, being righteous and sinless, deserved no suffering at all. He underwent guilt vicariously for His people. He not only suffered in His body to the point of death, but, in His human soul, He endured the infinite wrath of God. His human nature endured the divine forsakenness without being destroyed because it was sustained by His divine person who can never die. He was delivered up for our offenses and delivered because of justification, our justification having been thereby accomplished and His own as well (who had to be justified of the guilt He vicariously assumed). Had He been destroyed, He would not have been justified; nor would His people, for whom He would have died in vain.

Christ did not literally "descend into hell" nor to a *limbus patrum* which does not exist, nor to a Gehenna

Jesus' Teaching About Hell

which does. It was utterly unnecessary because the merit of His sacrifice delivered His guilt-laden human nature and His people's as well. He "descended" into the eternal punishment of Gehenna by receiving God's wrath in His perfect human nature. This was the equivalent - and more - of the penalty and punishment endured by sinners in hell by virtue of the fact that it was God the Son who, by the community of attributes, died in that human nature.

If you wish all the biblical texts involved in these statements above, read Fudge in these pages being discussed. He and others seem to think that only individual biblical statements and not a systematic, theological articulation of them is necessary. But you will see that in spite of all the learned discussions of the many texts, no coherent explanation of the atonement is forthcoming simply because Fudge, and many of those he cites, cannot see the divine forest for the divine trees. This, I may say, is different from the Gehenna errors proper, where even the trees cannot be seen. Fudge is a diligent, learned, and reverent student of the Bible, but a poor theologian of the Bible. That is not the only, but a major, weakness of <u>The Fire that Consumes</u>.

CHAPTER 7
PAUL'S TEACHING ABOUT HELL

Bypassing Fudge's handling of numerous Pauline texts, I will consider his attempt to grasp the general meaning. Here is Paul's view of the destiny of the wicked's soul according to Fudge's understanding. It was taught in Paul's day that the soul dies, becoming extinct at the death of every person. This was the view which Plato and Paul opposed.

> On the other hand, Plato believed that some would be punished forever (or at least for a very long time after death). According to him, such reprobate souls can continue in misery because they posess 'immortality,' are 'indestructible,' and 'immortal.' Yet, Constable affirms, 'not one of these terms is ever used in the New Testament to describe the future conditions of the lost. Let our opponents, whether they follow Augustine or Origen, show us but one such term applied to the wicked, and we will allow that we are wrong.'

E. White, R.F. Weymouth and Fudge continue Constable's challenge to Orthodoxy. While not admitting that this challenge has never been met by Orthodoxy in the past, as Fudge maintains, I will address it here.

First, I note that it is not necessary to find any

Paul's Teaching About Hell

particular doctrines in Paul. If it could be shown that Paul did not teach endless punishment, that would not prove that the Word of God does not teach it. Furthermore, by the principle in 2 Tim.3:16, Paul endorses everything taught by Scripture anywhere. If, then, the Bible anywhere teaches endless punishment, Paul teaches endless punishment.

Second, controversies can never be settled by words alone. What words mean in the context studied is significant. It is possible that Constable and others are quite correct in saying Paul used common language others used for extinction and did not use language they used for a period of suffering. That does not prove that Paul therefore taught the extinction of the wicked at death or did not teach their continuance in a state of suffering. Paul could avoid the usual language but express the concept or use the same language in a different meaning. The only cogency in Constable *et al*'s argument is that Paul may have taught an "unorthodox" doctrine and may have rejected the "orthodox" doctrine. That would remain to be seen by a study of his actual doctrine. In and of itself, Constable's is an observation, not an argument.

Third, it can be shown that Paul did teach the doctrine of Orthodoxy and not the conditionalist's view. Perhaps the best way to show that here is to examine the Pauline texts which Dr. Fudge has

Paul's Teaching About Hell

presented and show that they do not teach what Fudge has said, but their very opposite. For space's sake, the reader will allow me to limit myself to three important texts.

2 Thessalonians 1:5-10:

> 5. This is a plain indication of God's righteous judgment so that you may be considered worthy of the kingdom of God, for which indeed you are suffering.
> 6. For after all it is only just for God to repay with affliction those who afflicted you.
> 7. and to give relief to you who are afflicted and to us as well when the Lord Jesus shall be revealed from heaven with His mighty angels in flaming fire,
> 8. dealing out retribution to those who do not know God and to those who do not obey the gospel of our Lord Jesus.
> 9. And these will pay the penalty of eternal destruction, away from the presence of the Lord and from the glory of His power,
> 10. when He comes to be glorified in His saints on that day, and to be marveled at among all who have believed. (NASB)

Please note: (1) God is to *"repay with affliction"* (v.6). Extermination is not affliction; it is the prevention of affliction. Extermination is not an "equivalence of affliction." As we have shown repayment

Paul's Teaching About Hell

must go on forever for the wicked will continue to sin as they resent the "payment" and hate the Judge. The "last cent" is never going to be paid.

Note (2): this repayment is to occur at the Lord's return *"with His mighty angels in flaming fire, dealing out retribution..."* (v.7, 8). This, Christ says in Matthew 25:46, will result in the wicked going in to "everlasting punishment." Manifestly, He will do then what He said here. This "retribution" cannot be annihilation either at Christ's return or afterward for annihilation is not retribution. Dr. Fudge may not agree with the Westminster Shorter Catechism which teaches what the Scripture teaches, that every sin deserves eternal punishment. However, he must see that the wicked will be wicked still (Rev.22:11-15) and God will never be mocked, for whatever a man sows he will reap (Gal.5:21; 6:7, 8).

Note (3): though we have already seen that this repayment and retribution must be eternal, Paul does not leave the matter to implication. Explicitly he mentions "eternal destruction." Nothing is a greater mockery of "eternal destruction" than to say that it is an instantaneous or quick destruction that leaves eternal nothingness.

Note (4): this punishment puts the wicked "away from the presence of the Lord and from the glory of His power" (v.9). It is hardly a way to describe non-

Paul's Teaching About Hell

existent beings as *"away from the presence of the Lord and from the glory of His power."* Annihilated wicked men are neither near nor far from the Lord or anything. They do not exist. They are not anything or anywhere.

The "presence of the Lord" here is His favorable loving presence as He manifests Himself to His saints and is admired by them (v.10). The wicked will never be in that company to behold that aspect of the divine being (or they will never see it as such). They will be being eternally destroyed by His presence in wrath. God is despised by those who disbelieve. They hate His holy majesty. And they will be "away from <u>that</u> presence of the Lord" as long as it is manifested to His saints; that is, forever.

Note (5): there seems to be an implied parallelism here between the one scene where the Lord is graciously present and affectionately admired while in the other He is wrathfully present and hated for all the excellencies the saints admire in Him. Eternal life and eternal death; eternal love and eternal hatred; eternal joy and eternal misery.

For the conditionalists there is only one picture: ever- rejoicing saints and non-existent sinners. God is glorified in the vessels of mercy but not by the vessels of wrath. The righteous were made for the day of redemption but sinners were not made for the day

Paul's Teaching About Hell

of evil. (Prov.16:14) They were made for extinction; for nothing. It is is not like the divine Creator to have something He has created return to Him void. (Is.55:11) The "sons of perdition" were made for perdition, not extinction.

Yet Fudge could write that "Nothing in the language here requires or even clearly suggests conscious unending torment." (250) He is even comfortable with the notion that the wicked "will perish, be destroyed, be burned up, be gone forever...creation returns to chaos!"

That is what is wrong. Human creation did not come from chaos and it does not return to chaos. It came from God and must return to Him:

> ...all who are in the tombs will hear His voice and come forth, those who have done good, to the resurrection of life, and those who have done evil, to the resurrection of judgment. (John 5:28, 29)
> The spirit will return to God who gave it.
> (Ecc. 12:7)

Nothing returns to God void. No one fails to return to God who made him to receive what he deserves, either everlasting life in Christ his Savior or everlasting death in his chosen sin. Galatians 1:8,9:

Paul's Teaching About Hell

8. But even though we, or an angel from heaven, should preach to you a gospel contrary to that which we have preached to you, let him be accursed. (Not annihilated)
9. As we have said before, so I say again now, if any man is preaching to you a gospel contrary to that which you have received, let him be be accursed. (Not annihilated)

The NIV has "eternally condemned" for "accursed" and Fudge remarks that this is "interpretive though it is probably correct." (252) Since Fudge accepts this I will not try to prove it highly likely. All translation is "interpretive" to some degree. Translators differ as more or less interpretive not as interpreters or non-interpreters. A word can never be exactly defined by a dictionary for it is always in a context which the dictionary cannot anticipate exactly. Lexicons may limit the realm of possibilities but no more than that. The reader will notice throughout Fudge's book and this one, an on-going effort to understand words in context.

Here, we are agreed, Paul is saying that preachers of another gospel are to be eternally condemned. Fudge interprets the eternal condemnation as meaning that those who declare another gospel shall be relatively soon annihilated. I say the text imprecates them and calls for a punishment that lasts eternally.

Paul's Teaching About Hell

Who is correct? Fudge cannot be correct because his interpretation is actually meaningless and Paul's statement, we both agree, cannot be meaningless. A person is not being condemned eternally who does not exist eternally. Fudge's wicked do not exist eternally but have their existence extinguished for eternity.

This is an either/or situation. Either the wicked are eternally condemned or they are not eternally condemned. Fudge's wicked are not eternally condemned. Almost from the very issuance of the judgment of their condemnation they cease to exist and thus are incapable of eternal or any future condemnation. As I said, it is like a man dying of a heart attack whose torturers just start to work on him.

One may interject, that is their condemnation: to be extinguished, annihilated. They could be appointed to annihilation after serving their purpose as animals do to non-existence. But they cannot be <u>sentenced</u> to <u>eternal condemnation</u> by <u>annihilation</u>. They cannot really be rewarded or punished by non-existence. They may be praised by reward or punished by pain. Being moral beings, man must be rewarded or punished. He is no mere animal to be terminated.

I am not forgetting that Fudge poses as an exegetical Houdini. He can make an "eternal condemnation" into no condemnation by linguistic legerdemain. The condemnation destroys the person and this non-

Paul's Teaching About Hell

son exists eternally as a non-person and thus he, the non-person, is eternally condemned. Look, this rube says to the sophisticate, the person does have to exist to be eternally condemned. Your condemned person is not a person but a state of non-existence.

The expression "eternally destroyed" could convey the idea of being destroyed forever but even that is ambiguous. If a person meant to express Fudge's idea, it is easy but awkward. Simply say that a person will be annihilated and never, ever in eternity be brought into being again. Of course, the concept still defies comprehension because if the person is annihilated, that same person can't be brought into being again.

"Eternally condemned" has to mean condemned eternally for there is no intelligible way of construing it but as meaning condemned in a way that goes on eternally. One would have to say that such a person is condemned and that condemnation will never be withdrawn in eternity. That would not only be awkward but rather insipid. The sentence to condemnation would go on eternally but nothing would be said about the actual condemnation that was sentenced. The person sentenced to condemnation would be unaffected though his sentence went on eternally.

Fudge concludes that "there is no good reason, therefore, not to take Paul's primary words in their

Paul's Teaching About Hell

most ordinary and common senses. He says that the wicked will 'perish,' 'die,' be 'corrupted,' or be 'destroyed.'" (257)

This is a *non sequitur*:
1. "Perish," "die," "destroy" usually mean terminated existence.
2. Souls are not immune to having their existence terminated by God.
3. Therefore, these Pauline words mean the soul's terminated existence in "hell" (not its eternal duration in hell).

Only premise #1 is correct. Premise #2 is false because, as such, men are moral agents who must be rewarded or punished, not terminated without either. The conclusion #3 does not necessarily follow from the preceding premises. The conclusion should read: Therefore, these Pauline words may mean the soul's terminated existence in "hell," but that is assuming that premise #2 is correct.

What this whole lengthy discussion of Fudge really proves is that mere terms themselves do not settle the argument between temporal duration and eternal duration. The question is what the texts say that God will do. That is not settled by mere word studies but by the contextual meanings of the words. Also, theological ideas are relevant. Morally speak-

Paul's Teaching About Hell

ing, God can only punish infinitely, as shown. That means in hell eternally, or on the cross in the infinite sacrifice of the Son of God.

The conditionalists say that the words must be taken literally. Traditionalists say that the contextual meaning of the words show that they do not have their usual, literal meanings but indicate eternal perishing, eternal death, and eternal destruction.

Fudge makes an argument where there is no argument. Shedd makes a hypothetical argument where there _may_ be an argument. That is, Fudge simply asserts that these words mean what he says they mean. Shedd argues that they mean eternal perishing, not only because that is compatible with general Bible teaching, but because the context points to punishment, and extinction is no punishment. Therefore, the soul must exist eternally to be punished eternally.

The reader must judge for himself whether the traditionalist argument here is sound or not. But it is an argument. The traditionalist gives an argument versus the conditionalist's non-argument. The argument may be sound or unsound in the reader's judgment, but it is an argument. We traditionalists believe we have _proven_ the argument. The reader must decide that for himself. Fudge does not here offer an argument to consider.

Romans 2:6-11: God:

Paul's Teaching About Hell

> will give to each person according to what he has done. To those who by persistence in doing good seek glory, honor and immortality, He will give eternal life. But for those who are self-seeking and who reject the truth and follow evil, there will be wrath and anger. There will be trouble and distress for every human being who does evil: first for the Jews, then for the Gentile; but glory, honor and peace for everyone who does good: first for the Jew, then for the Gentile. For God does not show favoritism.

Fudge comments: "along with ...(2 Thess.1:6-10), these verses contain Paul's most detailed teaching concerning the fate of the lost." (261) I remember the doublet of sermons that Edwards has on these verses constituting the longest sermonic description he ever gave of "The Portion of the Wicked" and "The Portion of the Righteous." In the former series he includes eternal damnation in "The Portion of the Wicked," simply assuming that the "wrath and anger, trouble and distress" find their climax in hell. I do not remember his claiming that this particular text explicitly so states. I do not myself think this text in itself proves either the traditionalist or conditionalist view of future judgment, but would, of course, include whatever is taught elsewhere by Scripture. Except, I repeat, that "wrath and anger, trouble and distress" infer God's

Paul's Teaching About Hell

judgment which, in the nature of the case, must be unending in the world to come.

Fudge, however, claims this text and all of Paul for the conditionalists:

> Not once in this passage does he (Paul) mention everlasting torment. Immortality for him is always God's gift to the saved, as are incorruption, glory, honor and eternal life. Like Jesus before him, Paul freely borrows from the Old Testament's prophetic vocabulary. Also like Jesus, he adds to the Old Testament picture - not gory details of unending tortures, as did some of his contemporaries and many of his successors, but the shining, single beam of the gospel. Illuminated most brightly in that light is the figure of Jesus Himself. Jesus, not lurid details of conscious torment, is the contribution the New Testament makes to the Old Testament's apocalyptic literature. The cross has replaced the Valley of Hinnom as the best picture of God's wrath. In advance of the cross, Jesus spoke of His death in guarded terms and used the intertestamental term "Gehenna" of the fate of the wicked. After the cross, however, and the descent of the Spirit of Pentecost, no New Testament writer ever again uses that phrase of final punishment. Paul, who says more on the subject by far than any of the others, points continually to Jesus' death as its clearest revelation. With the death and resurrection of Jesus, judgment day has already begun. The gospel "reveals" it to men and women everywhere.

Paul's Teaching About Hell

It is God's last call to repent! (263)

No, Paul does not mention "everlasting torment," but neither does he exclude it. Fudge will admit that if it is the teaching of Scripture it is implicitly included. "Immortality for him (Paul) is <u>always</u> God's gift to the saved...." Where did Paul say that? "Also like Jesus, he adds to the Old Testament picture - not gory details of unending torture, as did some of his contemporaries and many of his successors." True, but if Jesus and Paul taught an eternal hell they gave enough "gory" detail. "...but the shining, single beam of the gospel." "But" should read "as well as."

> Illuminated most brightly in that light is the figure of Jesus Himself; Jesus, not lurid details of conscious torment, is the contribution the New Testament makes to the Old Testament's apocalyptic literature.

This is sheer, gratuitous, pejorative rhetoric, as any sensitive conditionalist must admit.

The cross has "not <u>displaced</u> the Valley of Hinnom as the best picture of God's wrath," except for those for whom Christ "descended" into the Valley of Hinnom. But it is true that the cross is the best "picture of God's wrath." Gehenna is only an imperfect one, which is the reason it must go on forever, while Christ

Paul's Teaching About Hell

died only once.

Likewise, for the rest of this statement of Fudge, a mixture of beautiful truth with horrible distortion. In making the cross a <u>displacement</u> of Gehenna when it is <u>deliverance</u> from it of all who believe and only such, Fudge touches bottom.

The treatment of "final punishment in the rest of the New Testament" (271) is much as expected. I will make only a few rather miscellaneous remarks. All the references to judgment here being construed in conditionalist terms are essentially meagre in comparison not only to true hell, but even to an ordinary worldling's earthly existence. Fudge justifiably observes the terror of anticipating death in <u>Les Miserables</u>, <u>Uncle Tom's Cabin</u>, <u>Roots</u>, and <u>Crime and Punishment</u> (275), but they are as nothing compared to the traditional hell and relatively little punishment for a <u>lifetime</u> of sin.

While discussing 2 Peter, Fudge returns to an important point: the continuance of sin after the death of the body:

> Peter gives three great examples to illustrate the certainty of his warning. Two of them we examined at length while considering the Old Testament - namely, the Flood, which destroyed the old world (v.5), and the destruction of Sodom and Gomorrah by fire from heaven (v.6). Throughout the Bible we

Paul's Teaching About Hell

> have found these two events mentioned time after time, standard and favorite prototypes of God's judgment against sin. Each case involved a total destruction with sinners exterminated and their sinful way of life annihilated forever. When evil doers obstinately refused to turn loose their wickedness even with God's judgment beating at the door, God had no other choice: sin and sinners must perish together. (This is a thought worth pondering when someone suggests that sinners in hell will continue to sin forever, so that both sin and sinners are eternal, only out of sight). (282-283)

Indeed, the Flood and the destruction of Sodom and Gomorrah were final temporal events, but Orthodoxy sees the Bible as teaching that they were <u>types</u> of final and eternal destruction (2 Peter 2; Jude 7 and elsewhere). I know that Fudge does not accept the orthodox interpretation, but he knows the orthodox have often "pondered" his type of thought and rejected it. Furthermore, Scripture is explicit that "evil doers" continue after death "obstinately" to refuse "to turn loose their wickedness" in hell. Compare Dives in Hades (Luke 16:22-28). Revelation 21:27 says of the New Jerusalem above that *"nothing unclean and no one who <u>practices</u> abomination and lying shall come into it..."* (emphasis mine).

Let me comment particularly on the concluding sentence: "This is a thought worth pondering when

Paul's Teaching About Hell

someone suggests that sinners in hell will continue to sin forever, so that both sin and sinners are eternal, only out of sight.)" Of course, Fudge is gratuitously assuming (indeed begging the question), that "perish" means pass into non-existence. Such a thought would destroy heaven which would suffer the misery of thinking God is unjust in acquitting the guilty rather than punishing them. In fact, Father Abraham and Lazarus are perfectly blessed while fully aware of the torments of Dives (Luke 16:20f.). The saints rejoice while the smoke of burning ascends (Rev.14:11).

Fudge comments on the angels, their punishment, and the punishment of men:

> As a third illustration of God's ability to hold the ungodly for judgment Peter cites the fallen angels. God sent them to "hell," where they are held in "gloomy dungeons" for judgment. These fallen angels held special fascination for certain apocalyptic writers between testaments; we observed several references to them in the books attributed to Enoch. Peter appears to reflect this literature more than once, and Jude quotes Enoch by name (Jude 14,15). Peter probably has the fallen angels in mind when he writes of the "spirits in prison" in his first Epistle (I Pet.3:19,20,22). He literally says here that they are kept in Tartarus, for which most English versions strangely put "hell." The word appears only once in Scripture, here borrowed from the literature of classical Greek. In the

Paul's Teaching About Hell

> Odyssey (11.575) Homer makes Tartarus the place where the Titans were enchained for endless punishment. Both Homer and Plato also call the place Hades, which is the Septuagint's usual choice in translating the Hebrew sheol.
>
> Whatever one might make of this passage and the angels in Tartarus, it adds nothing to our understanding of the final doom of human sinners, since (1) it concerns angels, not men, and (2) it speaks of detention before the judgment, rather than the punishment following.
>
> After a description of the pseudo-teachers' crimes, Peter returns to their punishment. Like brute beasts "born only to be caught and destroyed," these men too "will perish" (v.12). Both 'destroy' and 'perish' translate the same word (*phthora*, see Gal.6:8). Peter pictures brute beasts and wicked men coming to the final end, though the men must face first God's judgment, sentence and consuming fire. "Blackest darkness is reserved for them" (v.17). Jude completes the simile, comparing the spurious teachers to "wandering stars, for whom blackest darkness has been reserved forever" (Jude 13).

Strangely, Fudge thinks it strange that English versions translate Tartarus as hell when that is the way the Greeks themselves used that Greek word. Furthermore, this does add something to our understanding of the punishment of angels and men because Christ also says that those humans who go away to "everlasting punishment" go to the hell of fire "prepared for the

Paul's Teaching About Hell

devil and his angels."(Matthew 25:41) Also, even when the angels suffer "detention before judgment," they are kept in "eternal chains." (Jude 7)

A minor detail of Fudge's conditionalist interpretation of the "rising smoke" of Revelation 14:9-11:

> *If anyone worships the beast and his image and receives his mark on the forehead or on the hand, he, too, will drink of the wine of God's fury, which has been poured full strength into the cup of His wrath. He will be tormented with burning sulfur in the presence of the holy angels and of the Lamb. And the smoke of their torment rises for ever and ever. There is no rest day or night.*

Our author has often stressed the finality of the destroying by fire even though Isaiah and Christ speak of the fire which is not quenched. Here "the smoke of their torment rises for ever and ever. There is no rest day or night." That would seem to be plain enough even for a conditionalist. But not so:

> In saying the smoke "will rise forever," the prophet evidently means what he goes on to describe in the rest of the chapter. So long as time goes on, nothing will remain at the site but the smoke of what once

Paul's Teaching About Hell

> was Edom's proud kingdom. Again the picture of destruction by fire overlaps that of slaughter by sword (vv.17). The wicked die a tormented death; the smoke reminds all onlookers that the Sovereign God has the last word. That the smoke lingers forever in the air means that the judgment's message will never become out of date! (288)

Fudge, as John Stott did, says everything but the obvious: THE SMOKE RISES FOR EVER AND EVER BECAUSE THE FIRE MUST BE BURNING FOR EVER AND EVER. According to the Apostle John, "There is no rest day or night," but, according to the conditionalist, there is the rest of non-existence forever and ever. Needless to say, Fudge's "The Lake of Fire" is going to be a pool for summer vacationers - the death of death. (301f.)

Of Fudge's interesting survey of church historical discussion, I will note only two points, since only Scripture is infallible. First, let us look at "Augustine's Discussion of Final Punishment" and "Traditionalism's Problem of Pain."

Augustine's view of final punishment is considered in an appendix. It shows that Augustine in <u>The City of God</u> defends the orthodox doctrine of hell against the pagans, philosophically and biblically. The editors of Augustine's work, in addition to their brief summary, give their own critique of Augustine's

Paul's Teaching About Hell

way of arguing, assuming Plato's view which they find essentially faulty. First, they reject Plato and Augustine's immortality of the soul doctrine. Second, when arguing biblically, Augustine does not refer to the Old Testament or the way the Bible uses terms like "worms which do not die" and "unquenchable fire." Nor does he even consider the possibility of extinction though he must have been aware of that interpretation. The commentators follow Fudge's type of interpretation.

My reply: First, if the commentators were right they would only have shown weaknesses in Augustine's argument. Even if they had refuted him, which they did not attempt, Orthodoxy would not have been annihilated. Second, if Plato's doctrine of an immortal soul is wrong and Augustine agrees with it, his case for the immortality of the soul rests not on Plato, but on Scripture; namely that bodies and souls can be and will be made immortal by God. Third, Augustine thinks and shows that the Son of God teaches the orthodox doctrine. Fourth, likewise, he need not explicitly critique the theory of the extinction of persons in hell when he cites Scripture to show that they will be punished forever. He extinguishes extinction implicitly each time he proves eternal existence. Fifth, all that Appendix A <u>proves</u> is that some other scholars think as Fudge does, at least at certain points.

Paul's Teaching About Hell

Fudge's comments on "Traditionalism's Problem of Pain" (chapter 19) give this traditionalist no little pain. It early on makes this important concession about Orthodoxy's common belief:

> About all one can count on from traditionalist authors is that they believe that the wicked will remain alive forever, in sensible punishment of some description, so that neither they nor it will ever pass away. (412)

I could have wished that he had added that all the traditionalists believe this to be the indubitable teaching of Scripture, especially of Jesus Christ. The rest of the chapter is devoted to the different ways eternal punishment is depicted by different orthodox teachers with Fudge gratuitously inserting his view that they are all wrong. What he could then have said of the orthodox is that, if they are right, it is impossible to approach, much less exaggerate, the horrors of hell.

One word from Christ alone is sufficient to prove that the punishment of the wicked will be everlasting. If there were no other text in all Scripture teaching the awful doctrine, Matthew 25:46 would be enough to establish everlasting punishment everlastingly. At first glance, it is obvious this is what Jesus meant. At second glance, it is more obvious that this is what Jesus

Paul's Teaching About Hell

meant. At third glance, it is most obvious that this is what Jesus meant. At all glances, Jesus is telling us in Matthew 25:46 what He said in Matthew 23:33: this viperish generation cannot "<u>escape</u> the damnation of hell" by annihilation or by exhaustion. My little book has tried to prove that this is what Jesus and the Bible teach everywhere. "The fire that consumes," must consume forever because it is never quenched.

How many times must Christ say what He need have said only once? His Word surely abides forever and, if it does, sinners abide in hell forever. If they are ever annihilated, He and His word are annihilated with them. This is the reason I wrote this book. Not because I love hell and hate its annihilation, but because I hate attempts to annihilate God and His Son, Jesus Christ.

I make that last statement knowing that many - even traditionalists - will resent it. They will hasten to say that annihilationists may be wrong but many of them honestly think that they are biblical. Many of them love God and His Son, Jesus Christ, as much as any traditionalist. You, Gerstner, ought never to say that they are attempting to annihilate God. Shame!

I did not say that all annihilationists were <u>deliberately</u> attempting to annihilate God and His Son, Jesus Christ. I did say that Annihilationism attempts just that.

I feel that way about Dr. Fudge, whom I have never

Paul's Teaching About Hell

met. I think he thinks that he is honoring God and His Son and His Word. I am trying to convince him and others that their teaching, being contrary to Scripture, amounts to an attempt to annihilate God by saying that our holy God will annihilate rather than punish impenitent sinners. God will not allow men to mock Him (Gal.6:7), but, according to the annihilationist, He mocks Himself.

Severity and charity must be forthcoming from both sides so that we all remember always that since one of the conflicting sides must be wrong <u>one of us</u> is attempting to annihilate God by annihilating His Word, which cannot err or contradict itself or Himself. It is no casual matter to err in God's Word, certainly not on doctrines concerning future, eternal existence. Even here there are differences of degree in error. It is a great error to say that God will eternally punish the impenitent if He will not. It is a much greater error to say that He will not if He will.

Why? Because the difference in the consequences of the two errors is so very great. If God does not punish eternally, we traditionalists have made people anticipate a future for unbelievers far, far graver than it is. The wicked after death are going to be greatly relieved to learn that they are going to pass into oblivion rather than endure endless torment. If they have time, they will probably curse us traditionalists

Paul's Teaching About Hell

for causing them some unnecessary anxiety while they were still in this world.

If, however, the impenitent learn that they are not to be annihilated but eternally tormented every day, they will spend eternity cursing the annihilationists. These miserable persons will say that they might have sought conversion while they had opportunity had they realized that such a dread future awaited the unconverted. Undoubtedly, the lost will be cursing the erring annihilationists an eternity longer in hell than they would be the erring traditionalists, from oblivion.

Nor can there be any doubt which doctrine is more likely to set a sinner seeking repentance of the Lord while He may be found.

CHAPTER 8
THE DAY OF JUDGMENT, HEAVEN AND HELL

How does one feel about the Day of Judgment? If a person is still in his sins, Judgment Day is the Day of the Terror of the Lord. If he is saved in Christ Jesus, how eagerly will he anticipate that Day!

But godly Christians often shrink from the Day of Judgment. Yet there need be no fear - just the opposite. For Christians, it will be a greater day than the Day of the Lord. It will be the day of their Savior's Judgment. Our Lord will be the Judge of that day (Acts 17:31). And our Lord, our Judge, is also our Savior. The Day of Judgment will be the Day of Salvation: complete, perfect, body and soul. How eagerly Christians should expect the coming of Christ because it will be the Day of Judgment, the Day of Vindication.

The Christian's Day of Condemnation was passed when he first bowed to the Lord in repentance and faith. *"Neither do I condemn thee, go and sin no more."* (John 8:11) *"Now there is no condemnation for those who are in Christ Jesus."* (Rom.8:1) When Jesus Christ sits on that Throne of Judgment, His only word to His people will be, *"Come you blessed of My Father, inherit the kingdom prepared for you before the foundation of the world."* (Matt.25:34)

The Day of Judgment: Heaven and Hell

Oh yes, all things hidden will be revealed at the Day of Judgment (Rom.2:16). But believers' sins will be revealed as <u>forgiven</u> and their faithfulness will receive "rewards." The wicked's sins, too, will be revealed - as unforgiven! And all <u>their</u> deeds rewarded with endless punishment.

Until that day God's people cry, *"How long, O Lord, How long?"* (Rev.6:10) Then all is settled. All the injustices - every last one of them - settled justly forever.

> LIKE THE DRIVEN CHAFF THE WICKED
> SHALL BE SWEPT FROM OFF THE LAND
> WITH THE RIGHTEOUS THEY SHALL NOT
>   GATHER
> NEITHER IN THE JUDGMENT STAND.
> WELL THE LORD SHALL GUARD THE
>   RIGHTEOUS
> FOR THEIR WAY TO HIM IS KNOWN.
> BUT THE WAY OF EVIL-DOERS
> SHALL BY HIM BE OVERTHROWN. (Ps.1:5,6)

Man is spiritually D.O.A. (Dead On Arrival) in this world (Eph.2:1; John 8:34; Gen.6:5). Hell is where Satan rules and he rules over man in this world (I John 5:19). Man is called his "goods" (Mark 3:27). He is called a S.O.D. (Son of the Devil) by Jesus Christ (John 8:44). He serves the devil day and night without ceasing (Eph.2:2).

The Day of Judgment: Heaven and Hell

The terror of the Lord comes when man dies unregenerate, remaining the hellish creature he is here (Rev.22:11) with these differences:

1. There is no possible deliverance from eternal hell ever (Matt.25:46).
2. There is no relief. In this world the amusing diversions are so diverting that Satan's victims do not realize that all they are doing is gathering fuel for their ever more intense eternal burning (Rom.2:4).
3. The devil's complete fury is unleashed because he needs no longer waste any time diverting his victims' attention from a possible salvation (I Pet.5:8).
4. Worst of all, it is the wrath of God that is <u>poured out</u> (John 3:36) through Him and beyond Him for the impenitent.

Hell's misery is made perfect by the sight of the saints (whom they had despised and hated in this world in return for the saints' love of them and efforts for their salvation) enjoying everlasting bliss (Luke 16:23-26).

Those for whom heaven was prepared before the foundation of the world are nevertheless, because of the fall, born in hell's vestibule, this world. At the

The Day of Judgment: Heaven and Hell

divinely appointed time they are born again and enter the Kingdom of heaven (John 3:3-8). This world of tribulation becomes the vestibule of heaven for them. They begin "eternal life" here and now (John 3:16).

For the children of God there is no essential change at death. They now have Christ as their life. Sin "no longer reigns though it does remain" - John Murray. There it "remains" no longer. They see Christ and love Him perfectly (I John 3:6). Heaven is essentially the same there as here with these differences:

1. There is never any spiritual sin (Phil.1:6).
2. There is never any bodily pain (Rev.21:4).
3. They enjoy "life eternal" in its fulness, body and soul (John 5:29).
4. They have perfect love for themselves, their neighbors, and their God whom they now "see" (Matt.5:8).

Heaven's joy overflows as they see the wicked suffering their just desert from which the saints had so earnestly tried to save them in this world by begging them to believe on the Lord Jesus Christ and be saved (Rev.18:20). The just misery of hell serves its divine purpose of contributing to the happiness of the saints.

CHAPTER 9
WHO ARE GOING TO HELL AND WHO TO HEAVEN?

People are going to eternal hell every day by the thousands. Once recently, when I was in the hospital, I was in a bed alongside a man in constant misery frequently shrieking in torment. I could do nothing for the poor fellow but pray. At last his screaming stopped. He had died and gone to hell. There he will long through all eternity for the blessed comfort he enjoyed in that hospital bed where he died in pain.

I was later informed that the man who died next to me belonged to a religious group, association with which virtually guarantees a place in hell. Some people are in churches which allow their members to go to hell because they do not preach the gospel they profess. Other religious groups can guarantee hell because they do preach the false gospel they profess. Others have no gospel at all; an absolutely sure way to damnation. In Christian churches, many perish but there is always an outside possibility of salvation because the sacrament still preaches a gospel the administrators have forgotten; or a stray evangelist may say what the pastor no longer dares. But outside the church, one can be almost certain to perish.

The holocaust ordeal and death was the beginning,

Who Are Going to Hell

not the end, of misery for impenitent Jews, impenitent Jehovah's Witnesses, and impenitent <u>anyone else</u> who went from Auschwitz to eternal perdition which will never be escaped, even by death, ever. Why do we so much pity temporal, comparatively slight suffering (as we should), but ignore really terrible suffering?

As we survey the whole Christian scene, we see most "Christians" on their way to hell. On the world scene, all non-Christians - no exceptions - are on their way to hell. Of course, that cannot be true! It's my bigotry raising it ugly head. But you must know by now that it is not blind intolerance to say that those sinners who live and die without their sin's guilt being removed and its power broken must go to hell. "No one comes to the Father but by Me," says Jesus Christ.

No, they are not damned because they do not believe in Someone of whom they have never heard. They are damned because they are sinners. A holy God will never clear the guilty whether they have heard, or not heard, of a Savior. God condemns people for what they have done, not for what they have not done and could not do. He is a righteous God who will not clear the <u>guilty</u>. Innocents will never be condemned.

Infants are not innocent. You say, infants <u>cannot</u> be guilty. But you do not know infants. Jonathan Edwards said that they were little vipers. Augustine

And Who to Heaven?

said he was planning sins when he was on his mother's breast. More important, Scripture says that in <u>Adam all</u> died. (Rom.5:12f.) God destroyed Sodom and Gomorrah though it would have been saved if there had been "ten righteous." Surely the metropolis had ten little children. When the angel destroyed all the houses, the lintels of whose door did not have the blood sprinkled, many were infants. Infant Egyptians were unspared in God's holocaust.

According to the Bible, that is to say, according to God, we are all born D.O.A.'s and S.O.D.'s. We are <u>all</u> dead on arrival, sons of the devil. We are not talking of non-Christian D.O.A.'s and S.O.D.'s who never believe or hear of the Savior, but of everyone. Of course, all non-Christians are going to hell. But many who name the Name that is above every name will come under His judgment.

"Many know who do not say." If so, they are worse than those who do not know. Christians who do not proclaim the only Name given under heaven whereby men must be saved must be far worse than those who never know or believe the Name.

All impenitent pagans are going to hell, but the deepest places in the Pit will be reserved for impenitent "Christians." It will be more "tolerable" for pagans in hell than for all merely professing Christians.

But who are going to heaven? Every last one of

Who Are Going to Hell

you who repents and sincerely trusts in Jesus Christ as seen by your obedience. There is no hell for you because there was hell for Him.

"Repent or perish," says Jesus. I hope you are persuaded by now of what He means by perish and what He means by repent. In that case, the one great question before you, dear friend, is: "How to and How not to Repent."

CHAPTER 10
HOW TO AND HOW NOT TO REPENT

Please note that people are capable of misunderstanding the very title of this book, <u>Repent or Perish</u>. The title states that the reader must repent. Most people have a general idea of what "repent" means - a turning away from sin. It is the "you" that is likely to be misconstrued. Not the "you" but the "you repent." And not quite the "you repent," but what must happen that "you repent."

It is <u>not</u> your realizing how terrible hell is that leads "you to repent." People do not repent even when they are in hell and know by experience how terrible hell is. This little book may give you some idea of how terrible hell is, especially that it is everlasting. Jonathan Edwards makes anyone realize far better how terrible hell is. Jesus' saying these go away to "everlasting punishment" gives the most absolute sense of all how terrible hell is because He is the One who sends people there.

Nevertheless, the terribleness of hell has never made one soul repent. Even being there never will. Nothing will make you repent - not even you. Only God can cause you to repent and be saved. If He changes you, you will repent. If He does not, you will not.

How To And How Not To Repent

I did not write "Repent or Perish" thinking I could persuade you to repent. I am not that naive. I am not an Arminian fancying that I, by my writing, my preaching, my praying, can bring you to repentance. By the grace of God, I know better. I know that only God can lead you, or me, or anyone, to repent. Paul, who under divine inspiration wrote, *"knowing the terror of the Lord we persuade men"* (II Cor.5:11), explains how "we persuade" in First Corinthians 3:5-7:

> 5. Who then is Paul, and who is Apollos, but ministers by whom ye believed, even as the Lord gave to every man?
> 6. I have planted. Apollos watered; but God gave the increase.
> 7. So then neither is he that planteth any thing, neither he that watereth; but God that giveth the increase. (Emphasis mine)

When God changes you, you will repent. Not when He warns you, threatens you, pleads with you. He must change you if you are ever to repent. 2 Tim.2:24-26:

> 24. And the servant of the Lord must not strive; but be gentle unto all men, apt to teach, patient,
> 25. In meekness instructing those that oppose themselves; if God peradventure will give

How To And How Not To Repent

> them repentance to the acknowledging of the truth;
> 26. And that they may recover themselves out of the snare of the devil, who are taken captive by him at his will.

God must change you from inside out; from the heart out. He must give you a new heart. "You must be born again." (John 3:3) Then and only then will you hate sin, love Christ; turn from sin, turn to Christ. That is, only then will "you repent." And when you repent I will write another book for you if you wish: You Are Going to Heaven Unless You...Look Back. If you ever, having put your hand to the plow, turn back, you will show that you did not truly repent about your old heart. You were only sorry about it (Luke 9:62).

If only God can give repentance, why did I write Repent or Perish? I did write the book to get you to repent. You are going to hell unless...you repent. That is why I wrote the book. You must repent. If you really do not want to go to hell you will repent!

The point is that if you are going to repent and not go to hell, you have to have your impenitent heart changed. You need a penitent heart instead of the impenitent one you now have. Otherwise, all you can do now is say, "I repent." But that makes matters worse because you do not mean it. Your heart is impenitent. If you say otherwise, it is a lying heart.

How To And How Not To Repent

Saying "I repent" when you do not repent does not save you from hell. Saying "I repent" when you do not repent sinks you deeper into hell.

When you say "I repent" with your impenitent heart, this is what you mean: "I am sorry about going to hell. I do not want to go into a furnace of eternal fire. I shrink and shriek from the mere thought of being thrown into the fiery cauldron. I couldn't be anything but sorry about my fate if that is what awaits."

You see? You're not sorry about sin. You're only sorry about your suffering for your sin. Your old impenitent heart still loves its sin. It just doesn't love the consequences of it. It'll do anything to avoid hell. Hate and turn from its sin? Not that. Anything but that!

"I can't hate what I love. I love sin. I live in sin. I can't live without sin. I'd die without sin."

That is the truth. You will die eternally. You will die in hell rather than be without sin. Even hell's fires can't burn that love of sin out of you. You are getting your wish. Your love of sin will not be taken away. You will go where you can sin for all eternity and be with fellow-sinners all the time.

You do not repent of sin at all. Not for one sin you have ever committed or any you will ever commit. You may say that you do. You may seem to. You may give up some sinful things you do. But you will never,

How To And How Not To Repent

ever give up the love of them.

As long as you remain as you are now, you are going to love sin. Repentance is literally impossible for you. You cannot make yourself other than you are.

> Can the Ethiopian change his skin
> Or the leopard his spots?
> Then you also can do good
> Who are accustomed to do evil. (Jer.13:23)

You must be changed. If God gives you a penitent heart you will hate sin and you will really repent. You will say "I repent" and mean it. You are a new creature in Christ Jesus. You have a new heart. You, for the first time in your life, hate sin and not only the consequences of sin.

The strange thing is that you no longer hate the consequences of sin because you know that they are what sin deserves. You know a holy God must visit you with the consequences. And He does.

You are glad to have been punished and been threatened with eternal punishment. You know this is what sin deserves. You now hate sin and love its consequences. You used to love sin and hate its consequences. Now you hate sin and love its consequences. You stole some money and hated being detected and fined and maybe imprisoned. Now you return the money with interest and accept whatever

How To And How Not To Repent

further penalty the law requires.

You would even want to go to hell because that is what your sin deserves - except for one thing. The guilt of your sin has been suffered for by your Savior. God would not be holy and just if He punished you as if His Son had not "descended into hell" for you. Hell is the place where God's wrath burns forever, but there is no condemnation for you since Christ endured it for you. He has made you acceptable in the Beloved. (1 Pet.2:5) You don't want to go to hell because you <u>don't</u> deserve it anymore. You have Christ and His heaven which He has purchased for you with His blood.

This is the irony. The people who admit that hell is just do not go there. The people who do not admit it is just (because they are liars) are the ones who go there. This is the reason heaven rejoices in, rather than weeps over, hell. Heaven sees that this is where God punishes those who deserve to be punished in exactly the degree they deserve, eternally.

In its own way, hell is just like heaven. Heaven is the place where virtue, the infinite, perfect, righteousness of the Son of God, is rewarded to those who <u>by Christ deserve it</u> and in exactly the proper degree. Hell is the place where vice is given exactly what it deserves as far as that is possible. As we have seen, it is not possible for a finite being to receive the infinite

How To And How Not To Repent

wrath he deserves. So he must go on suffering forever because he will never have paid the "last cent" he owes.

We said all this and heaven follows "if you get a new heart." Let us see how to get a new heart which delivers you from hell and brings you to heaven.

We have seen that you, with your native impenitent heart, will never produce repentance. We have seen that you can say you repent but never mean it, and that such hypocrisy is only fuel for more burning. We have seen that only God can create a new heart within you. With that new heart you truly repent, turn from hell and toward heaven.

So the great question is, "How do I get God to give me a new heart?" The first answer is, "Ask Him, and you'll have it." But, alas, you only truly ask Him when you have it! You do not have it because <u>you</u> ask Him for it; you ask Him because you have it.

The reason is plain. You, with your impenitent heart, will never ask Him. You love sin and hate virtue. You can never ask for what you hate; <u>sincerely</u> ask. You can ask in the sense of saying the words; but, you'll never ask in the sense of meaning the words.

Remember you are an impenitent sinner. If you ever really desire virtue, you <u>have been</u> changed. I repeat: God changes you and only then with true repentance you truly thank Him for it.

How To And How Not To Repent

What, then, does an impenitent sinner do? Be honest! Admit to God, who knows you and your impenitent heart, that you hate Him and are not at all sorry about that. He knows it better than you, but acknowledging it is the first step you can make.

Acknowledge, too, that hell scares you but does not scare the hell out of you. You are running scared but still not repentant. You fooled yourself for awhile but no more. You never fooled God for a minute.

You love the sin that destroys you. But you sincerely hate pain; any pain. Eternal, immeasurable pain in body and soul? How you hate that! You hate that <u>almost</u> as much as you love the sin that drives you to it.

Remind God that He is the only one - least of all, yourself - who can take the love of sin away. Yet, you do not even want to have the love of sin taken away! You love sin and you love the love of sin. But you do not want to pay the price. Say: "I love sin, but it's not worth the price. God cure me. Change me. Make me a person who is not a lover of sin. I don't want to go to hell and suffer forever."

Don't pretend that you love God. Admit that you hate Him. You hate the One of whom you are asking this great favor. Admit you are sinning even as you ask Him. You are bowing low not because of respect, not to mention love. Admit that even your asking is sinful.

How To And How Not To Repent

You do not really want a new heart, all you want is to stay out of hell and that's the only way out. I have to ask the One who is sending me there, whom I hate. I must ask Him not to send me where I deserve to go. I admit even that reluctantly.

The only things I am sure of are two: (1) I am an impenitent sinner who hates God, and (2) He is the only One who can love and save me from hell!

It is not very promising. Even you will admit that. Hating God, even while you ask this supreme favor, you cannot expect to be fruitful. But this is the only possible way out of hell. It's a God I hate who will save me or no one.

> The Bible talks about grace, undeserved favor. That is what I am asking for. An infinite, undeserved favor. It is grace I am asking for. It is grace I need. It is mercy alone that can save me. Because it is mercy, I remember that God says: "I will have mercy on whom I will have mercy." (Rom.9:15) Yes, Lord, I want mercy but I cannot demand it. It is yours to give or not to give. I will wait it out.

> You may never give it, Lord. But I'm going to die begging. I don't deserve it. I deserve hell. But I need mercy. Mercy alone can save me.

> You may **not** give. You don't owe it. You don't owe me anything - except hell!

How To And How Not To Repent

> But you <u>may</u> give it. You say, '<u>I will have mercy</u> on on whom I will have mercy.' So you do show mercy to some. I beg to be among that some.
>
> I'm that widow who kept knocking until the judge, who didn't even want to be bothered, answered her for his sake if not for hers. I'm going to keep bothering you, <u>just</u> and <u>merciful</u> Judge, not for your justice but for your mercy, though you hate me, sinner that I am. Sinner that I am - even as I sinfully beg you for pardon.
>
> I'm like those soldiers you talked about, Jesus, who would take the Kingdom by whatever. That's the only hope I have. I'm going to keep storming heaven until you let me in, or I die in the attempt to be received. I'm pleading nothing but need. All that I have to offer is my misery and fear of greater misery. Have mercy on me, you sovereignly merciful God, I beg.

That is what you must do, my friend, if you are ever <u>possibly</u> to escape "the wrath that is to come."

There is great hope but no presumption. You dare not rest on your innocence or your excuses or your temptations. You do not rest on God's owing you any sympathy, not to think of pardon. You may not even rest on His mercy. He is sovereign in that. If you presume on anything, including the mercy of God, you will **NEVER** receive mercy.

How To And How Not To Repent

If you do not presume but only beg, there is HOPE. One day - tomorrow? Thirty years from now? You may get up from your knees a new creature in Christ Jesus! A new you with a penitent heart! But you may not, ever! God may still let you go to the hell you so richly deserve.

Do you explode with indignation? If so, this shows your begging was only a gesture after all. You really thought you had mercy coming to you. You earned mercy by all your begging.

To keep you on your knees until you are lifted by the grace of God or stand up in hell, let me show you there is no use hoping that hell will ever let you go as Dr. Fudge tries to prove. That book won't help. F.F. Bruce's foreward won't help. Clark Pinnock's saying this work has not been answered to his satisfaction won't help. It won't help that John Wenham does not believe in hell anymore. Philip Hughes has given up this point of faith, but it won't relieve you. Richard John Neuhaus says there is a hell, but no one is in it - a good way to gain entrance. Even the "Pope of the Evangelicals" himself, John Stott, can't save you.

Remember, trembling sinner, beg God for His sovereign mercy, apart from which you will encounter what the "fire that consumes" consumes: impenitent sinners eternally.

At the same time we turn in shame from our sinful

How To And How Not To Repent

selves (repentance), we turn to Christ (faith). The turning from one to the other is usually called "conversion." The turning is simultaneous as well as inseparable. One cannot turn to Christ in faith without turning from self in repentance.

A great theologian once asked a class of sixteen students which came first in conversion, faith or repentance. Eight were for faith; eight for repentance. Neither group was right or wrong. The two are simultaneous. Opposite sides of the same coin. Aspects of the same experience. When you are turning to Christ, you are turning from the world. When you are turning from the world, it is Christ to whom you are turning.

Faith can be separated from "faith." There are virtually a half-dozen experiences that go by the <u>name</u> <u>faith</u>. Only one is <u>saving</u> faith. There are also at least two experiences that go by the <u>name</u> repentance. Only one is <u>saving</u> repentance. The first is the sorrow of this world (II Cor.7:10). *"...worldly grief ("repentance") produces death."* It "produces death" because it is not a turning from sin, but merely from sin's consequences. It is a counterfeit repentance that sometimes passes for real. Esau had it (Heb.12:17), Ahithopel had it (II Sam.17:23), Judas had it (Acts 1:18-20).

"Repent or Perish ." Remember it must be true - not merely legal or nominal - repentance. And remember - only God can give it.

CHAPTER 11
DOES GOD LOVE THE SINNER AND HATE ONLY HIS SIN?

"Repent or Perish " forces people to ponder seriously the popular slogan, "God hates the sin and loves the sinner." Is a necessary repentance consistent with "God loves the sinner?" If God loves the sinner while he is alive, it is strange that God sends him to hell as soon as he dies. God loves the sinner to death? Loves him to everlasting torment?

There is something wrong here. Either God loves the sinner and will not send him into the furnace of His eternal wrath; or He sends him into His eternal wrath and does not love him. Either "you are going to hell unless" because God hates you, as you are. Or, God loves you and "you are going to hell unless" is false.

What leads almost everyone to believe that God loves the sinner is that God does the sinner so much good. He bestows so many favors including letting him continue to live. How can God let the sinner live and give him so many blessings, unless He loves him? There is a kind of love between God and sinners. We call it the "love of benevolence." That means the love of good will. *Benevolens* - willing well. Doing well. God can do well to the sinner without loving him with the other kind of love. "Complacent love," a pleasure

Does God Love the Sinner

in, affection for, admiration of. It exists in perfection between the Father and the Son, *"in whom I am well pleased"* (Matt.3:17; Mk.1:11).

God is perfectly displeased with the sinner. The sinner hates God, disobeys God, is ungrateful to God for all His favors, would kill God if he could. He is <u>dead</u> in trespasses and sins. (Eph.2:1) *"The thoughts and intents of his heart are only evil continually."* (Gen.6:5) He is the slave of sin (John 8:34), the servant of the devil, (Eph.2:2).

God has no complacent love for the sinner at all. He has a perfect hatred of him, *"I hate them with a perfect hatred."* (Ps.139:22)

Why does God do so much good for those He perfectly hates and as soon as they die impenitent send them immediately to hell and never in all eternity does them one solitary favor more? It is to show His willingness to forgive the sinner if only he will repent. It shows the sincerity of God's willingness to pardon the greatest sinner that, even while He hates him with a perfect hatred, He showers him with constant daily blessings.

As I mentioned in Chapter 1, there is no "problem of pain." The only problem is the "problem of pleasure." Dreadful as it is, it is not surprising that God sends sinners to hell. The problem is why He does not do it sooner. Why does God let a hell-deserving sinner

And Hate Only His Sin?

live a minute and then let him prosper like the green bay tree (Ps.37:35), as well? It is obvious that God can destroy the ungrateful. Why doesn't He? That is the problem.

Yes, the sinner suffers, too. But so little. It is a gentle reminder: though the sinner receives many divine favors, that does not mean that God is pleased with him. It is in spite of the fact that God hates him with a perfect hatred.

> Or do you think lightly of the riches of His kindness and forbearance and patience, not knowing that the kindness of God leads you to repentance? (Rom.2:4)

Our text also shows that the one reason a sinner is permitted to be born into and enjoy this world rather than wake up as an infant in hell is that God, with His love of benevolence, is determined to give the sinner a "chance," an opportunity to repent. Alas, most sinners use it as a chance to sin! They make God's blessed love of benevolence into a curse.

In this world the sinner enjoys nothing but the benevolent love of God. Every experience of pain as well as pleasure is from God's love - of benevolence. Even pain is from love because it tends to wake the sinner to his danger. God indeed loves the sinner, whom He hates with a perfect hatred, with a perfect love of benevolence.

Does God Love the Sinner

The sinner, as I said, makes every divine blessing into a curse including God's love of benevolence. This he does by construing a love of benevolence as a love of complacency.

Construing God's love of benevolence as a love of complacency is fatal. Instead of the divine forbearance leading to repentance, it is used as an excuse for non-repentance. Thus the sinner is not saved but damned by God's love of benevolence.

God "loves" the sinner benevolently and hates the sinner displacently. If the sinner dies impenitent, God removes His love of benevolence and pours out the full wrath of his displacent love.

As far as "hatred of sins" is concerned, sins do not exist apart from the sinner. God does hate sinning, killing, stealing, lying, lusting, etc., but this alludes to the perpetrator of these crimes.

God never hates the redeemed even when they sin. Is He an unfair respecter of persons? No! (Act.10:34) God hates the unredeemed sinner but loves the redeemed even when they sin for a good and just reason. God loves the redeemed even when they sin because His Son, in whom God is always well-pleased, ever lives to make intercession for them. (Rom.8:27,34) Christ died to atone for the guilt of His people's sins. When they sin, these are atoned-for sins. They are sins with their guilt removed. In one sense, they are not

And Hate Only His Sin?

sins at all. God does not hate His people when they sin because they are <u>in</u> His Son, Christ Jesus. And they are made <u>acceptable</u> in His Son. He *"has made us accepted in the Beloved."* (Eph.1:6)

Divine nepotism? No, His Son died for these people and paid the price for their sins past, present, and future. They are cancelled before they are committed. That is truth, not fiction. Righteousness, not nepotistic favoritism. In fact, it is not their original relationship to Christ which makes their sins guiltless, but Christ's making satisfaction for their sins that created the relationship as children adopted into the family of God.

God, in hot displeasure, chastens His people when they sin (Ps.6:1; 38:1). It is not hatred but complacent love in Christ Jesus. *"Whom the Lord <u>loves</u> He chastens."* (Heb. 12:6,7) God loves His people even when He afflicts them and hates the impenitent even when He befriends them.

Why the chastening when there is love? God blessed the wicked when there was holy hatred. Now He chastens His people when there is holy love. This is because true moral behavior must be perfected. No sin can be tolerated in those for whom Christ died. He died to purchase a *"peculiar people zealous of good works."* (Titus 2:14) Being redeemed, so far from tolerating their sinning, precludes it. Anyone who

Does God Love the Sinner

persists in sinning proves thereby that he is <u>not</u> a child of God. God punishes His own especially because they are His children. *"You only have I chosen among all the families of the earth: **Therefore** I will punish you for all your iniquities."* (Amos 3:2)

"Upright" man was promised and warned. A holy, just, and perfect God would promise and warn. Eternal life - if obedient. Instant death - the moment of disobedience. (Gen.3:5; Ecc.7:29)

When man sinned, he died spiritually and was rejected from communion with God his maker and friend. (Gen.3; Rom.5:12ff) The wrath of God was upon him; labor was his lot; suffering in child-birth; alienation and death, as threatened. God is holy; of purer eyes than to behold iniquity. (Hab.1:13)

Yet mortal man "lived" on (though to live in pleasure is death, 1 Tim.5:6), and so did promise. When the angels sinned they perished without delay, without promise, without hope.

Man's fate was better and worse than the fallen angels' lot. It was a day of possible salvation but also of possible greater damnation, greater damnation for sinning away the day of possible salvation. God in His wrath; God in His mercy; at the same time.

This was a terrible but holy wrath. God was using His omnipotent power but according to His perfect justice. Man was affected but he deserved it. It was

And Hate Only His Sin?

no more, no less, than he deserved. God is no more powerful than holy; no more holy than powerful.

As man continued to sin, God continued to increase His fury. His wrath is in no hurry. The record is kept, all accounts receivable. Every idle word will be brought into judgment (Matt.12:36). The cup of iniquity must be filled. Then wrath to the uttermost. (1 Thess.2:16) God's glory shines in the perfection of His work.

But - God decreed the sin, (Prov.16:4). Yes, for good and for glory. Man did it for evil and for shame.

A little sin and infinite wrath? A little sin against an infinite God is infinite. Wrath is in perfect proportion to the guilt. But even if the punishment were finite it would go in "infinitely," unendingly, because the sinner continues to sin in resenting it.

All glory to God for His holy anger. (John 17:3; Rom.9:17f)

CHAPTER 12
A HARD BOOK?

I know this is a hard book. Most people who read it will refuse to believe it. Be it right or wrong, they will refuse to believe it. That eliminates it for them now; but, alas, not forever.

Even some who agree with it may regret it. They will think that though it is biblical and true, it ought not to speak the hard truth. They will say that I turn people off. People will be hardened rather than won, they warn. You win more people with sugar....

They will put the blame on me. I do not mind. In fact, I would feel honored. But I do not deserve the credit. It is God's Word and He alone enabled me not to be offended and not to shrink from declaring the whole counsel of God as a faithful minister must. (Acts 20:19)

Maybe the book is too unrelenting, too "dogmatic," too everything. But really the important question is whether it is true as I have tried to show it is. If it is true, it must be spoken, written, preached, believed.

One who knows God's Word and does not warn sinners is letting them go to hell unhindered. They will perish, God says. But so will those who did not warn them! God says they will perish with them:

A Hard Book?

> Son of man, I have made thee a watchman unto the house of Israel: therefore hear the word at my mouth, and give them warning from me.
> (Ezekiel 3:17)

> I have appointed you a watchman for the house of Israel; so you will hear a message from My mouth, and give them warning from Me. When I say to the wicked, 'O wicked man, you shall surely die,' and you do not speak to warn the wicked from his way, that wicked man shall die in his iniquity, but <u>his blood I will require from your hand</u>.
> (Ezekiel 33:7-8)

I began this book by saying that people are going to hell daily by the thousands. Probably ministers and other witnesses who do not believe and, even worse, those who do but do not warn are going to hell daily by the tens if not hundreds. In comparison with such ministers, those who go to hell by the thousands will find hell "tolerable."

That paragraph will probably elicit more wrath from my peers than anything else in the book. "You mean to say that we're going to hell just because we don't believe in your hell and don't shout it from our pulpits and scare people out of their wits?"

Of course, it is not my hell, and I said nothing about shouting or scaring people out of their wits. Hell is meant to scare people **into** their wits. Awaken them to

A Hard Book?

consider their plight while something can be done. It is that or letting them be awakened by the flames and consider their plight when it is on them.

After all, if Paul was only free of the blood of men because he did not shrink from declaring the whole counsel of God (Acts 20:26-27), are we lesser mortals exempt? If people perish because of silent witnesses, we must perish with them. Hell is made for those supposedly solicitous of man who are disobedient to God. So far from saving men by not offending them with "hell-fire rantings," we will perish with them, having them add to our torture by damning our "tenderness" as long as they live in hell; that is, forever. Beware when all men speak well of you because they are not going to be praising you for their eternal damnation, even though you share it with them.

Proverbs 28:23 tells us that *"He who rebukes a man will afterward find more favor then he who flatters with the tongue."* The Proverb is referring to a good man who appreciates justified rebukes. Those in hell appreciate nothing. They will know as they see you praising God in heaven that you spoke the truth. But they won't thank you for it in hell, even though you tried to save them from going there. That is because they are ungrateful liars whose every word is a curse for everyone, especially themselves. But their minds will be intact in hell. They will know what

A Hard Book?

you did though they hate you for it. They will also know what their "friends" did and hate them even more.

In conclusion, let me remind you all there is a place worse than hell and better than heaven. This present world! Because, dear friends, if you are not born again you are now adding fuel for your eternal burning. That is worse than suffering hell now, because it makes hell more hellish when you go there forever. But, if you are born of God, everyday you live for Him you are adding treasures to your <u>eternal life</u> in heaven, making heaven more heavenly when you go there forever.

So I beg <u>all</u> of you: *"Seek the Lord while He may be found!"* (Isa.55:6) If, in fact, you do find Him, partly because of this feeble warning, I should be grateful to know of it. Even your vituperations will be respectfully considered.

Other Soli Deo Gloria Titles by John H. Gerstner

Theology for Everyman

The ABC's of Assurance

Jonathan Edwards, Evangelist

A Primer on Roman Catholicism

Reasons for Faith

Reasons for Duty

Dr. Gerstner was a contributing author to the book published by Soli Deo Gloria entitled *Justification by Faith ALONE!* His chapter was on the nature of saving faith.

Additionally, Soli Deo Gloria is publishing Dr. Gerstner's *Theology in Dialogue,* due out in July of 1996. This hardback book is a 25 chapter systematic theology done in question and answer form.

For a complete listing of titles, contact:

Soli Deo Gloria
P.O. Box 451, Morgan, PA 15064
(412) 221-1901/FAX 221-1902